The
Intrepid Parent's
FiELD GUiDE
to the
BABY
KiNGDOM

Adventures in Crying, Sleeping,
Teething, and Feeding for the
NEW MOM & DAD

JENNIFER BYRNE

Adamsmedia
Avon, Massachusetts

Published by
Adams Media, a division of F+W Media, Inc.
57 Littlefield Street, Avon, MA 02322. U.S.A.
www.adamsmedia.com

ISBN 10: 1-4405-5448-X
ISBN 13: 978-1-4405-5448-3
eISBN 10: 1-4405-5449-8
eISBN 13: 978-1-4405-5449-0

Printed in the United States of America.

10   9   8   7   6   5   4   3   2   1

Contains material adapted and abridged from *The Everything® Baby's First Year Book, 2nd Edition* by Marian Edelman Borden with Alison D. Schonwald, MD, FAAP, copyright © 2010, 2002 by F+W Media, Inc., ISBN 10: 1-60550-368-1, ISBN 13: 978-1-60550-368-4, and *The Everything® Father's First Year Book, 2nd Edition* by Vincent Iannelli, MD, copyright © 2010, 2005 by F+W Media, Inc., ISBN 10: 1-4405-0600-0, ISBN 13: 978-1-4405-0600-0.

This publication is designed to provide accurate and authoritative information with regard to the subject matter covered. It is sold with the understanding that the publisher is not engaged in rendering legal, accounting, or other professional advice. If legal advice or other expert assistance is required, the services of a competent professional person should be sought.

—From a *Declaration of Principles* jointly adopted by a
Committee of the American Bar Association and a
Committee of Publishers and Associations

Many of the designations used by manufacturers and sellers to distinguish their product are claimed as trademarks. Where those designations appear in this book and F+W Media was aware of a trademark claim, the designations have been printed with initial capital letters.

Illustrations by Eulala Conner.

*This book is available at quantity discounts for bulk purchases.
For information, please call 1-800-289-0963.*

CONTENTS

INTRODUCTION: Approach with Caution! 5

CHAPTER 1: Preparing the Nest 7

CHAPTER 2: Encountering the Wild Infant 17

CHAPTER 3: The Wild Infant at Rest 33

CHAPTER 4: Soothing Your Wild Infant's Cries 43

CHAPTER 5: Wild Breastcapades 55

CHAPTER 6: Formula for Success 77

CHAPTER 7: Babyius *MessiusSmellius* 91

CHAPTER 8: The Food Chain 109

CHAPTER 9: Grooming the Wild Infant 135

CHAPTER 10: Your Baby's Jaws 153

CHAPTER 11: Illness in the Wild 157

CHAPTER 12: Playtime 171

CHAPTER 13: Leaving the Jungle 187

CHAPTER 14: Communication Across Species 219

CHAPTER 15: Walking Upright 237

CONCLUSION: Year One, in the Books 249

APPENDIX: Resources 251

INDEX 253

*This book is dedicated to
my first "baby," Wally, with love.*

Introduction

APPROACH WITH CAUTION!

Hello, brave new parents! So, you've decided to embark on the amazing adventure of having a baby. That's great news! This journey is going to be exhilarating, surprising, hilarious, and terribly, terribly frightening.

You heard me—I said frightening. That's because your new baby will bear a shocking resemblance to a wild animal. One that's untamed, uncivilized, and utterly mysterious. A squirmy, regurgitating, unpredictable little creature. And it's not just the baby, either—your whole *life* will become a mystery to you. Just as if you ventured into the vast plains of the Serengeti, you'll be entering an entirely new ecosystem, with its own crazy set of rules.

For starters, your once-familiar landscape will become unrecognizable. Suddenly, your living room floor will be dotted with squeaky, blinky, potentially seizure-inducing toys, and your car's back seat will contain a car seat, mirrors, spilled Cheerios, and a cartoon-character sunshade. Your schedule will cease to have any logical structure—instead, your new wild infant will dictate who eats and when (FYI: you eat last, in case the suspense was killing you). Your attempts to leave your nest will be encumbered by brightly colored, Velcro-and-vacuum-equipped accessories—seriously, it's almost enough gear to start an entirely new village. Your ability to communicate with this wild infant will be almost nonexistent—his language skills are . . . let's say primitive, at best.

Watching your wild infant will be like observing a totally different species in its natural habitat—fascinating, mystifying, and very, very scary. Except unlike a visitor to a safari, you can't just put down your binoculars and walk away from this wild adventure. You can't just breathe a sigh of relief that the safari guides know how to use tranquilizers, and think, "Whew! I'm so glad that's not *my* job." Because it kind of is your job now. This wild creature is all yours.

That's where this book comes in. After all, if you visited the Serengeti, you'd bring a knowledgeable guide, right? You need a fellow explorer who's been there before and knows the lay of the land. Someone who can tell you which plants are safe to eat, share the most effective taming methods, and teach you the difference between the footprints of a wildebeest and the knee impressions of a wild human crawler. Someone who can school you in the endless varieties and consistencies of wild poop classification. No, that's not wild boar dung—that came out of your baby!

Gradually, over the first year, you'll adjust to your new ecosystem and its cycles and rhythms. At that point, your little wild animal will go from being a safari creature to being a fully integrated—and much beloved—member of your tribe.

So congratulations, good luck, and may God have mercy on your soul.

Chapter 1

PREPARING THE NEST

Welcome to the jungle! You have made the . . . let's call it *interesting* . . . choice to bring a wild infant (scientific name: *Kingdomius infantius*) into your personal habitat. Rest assured that your wild infant will bring you many hours of fascinating hijinks and memorable "events." Actually, you can rest assured that you will *not* rest assured for the foreseeable future. So you might as well make your nest as friendly and hospitable for all of you as possible.

THE INFANT'S PERSONAL NEST: HIS ROOM

Once you know that an infant will be soon arriving at your habitat, you're probably eager to design his or her room. Some *Kingdomius infantius* parents like to decorate the wild infant's bedroom in colors and designs specific to the future child's gender, provided that this information is available. Traditionally, the color pink and creatures such as flowers, kittens, and polka dots are associated with infants having female reproductive organs. The color blue and anything related to transportation vehicles, sports activities, or volunteer firefighting seem to be linked to infants having a wee-wee part. If you do not know the gender of your child, it seems that yellow and mint green occupies the hazy middle ground of gender neutrality, and giraffes are the official mascot of androgyny. So if you don't know your child's gender, just decorate the room with yellow and giraffes and hope for the best.

Remember, wild infants have incredibly poor eyesight at first, so he won't begin to resent your decorative neutering for several months. At that point, you can just draw a baseball cap (or high heels) on that giraffe, and call it a day.

A Nocturnal Habitat

Perhaps the first item you'll need for your revamped nest is a safe crib—which is ironic, as your baby might appear to sleep anywhere *except* her crib at first. This crib will not only be her sleeping quarters; she'll also spend plenty of time exploring (and chewing on) this environment as she grows.

Therefore, you need to look out for potential crib trouble on your crazy little offspring's behalf. You cannot simply look at her and say, "What on earth are you thinking? Your idea to gnaw on that crib slat was one of the most preposterous things I have ever seen. Did you really think you could actually digest this sustainable New Zealand pine?"

Here are some features a safe crib will include:

- A firm mattress with a tight-fitting crib sheet
- Slats that are not more than $2^{3}/_{8}$ inches apart
- No soft objects such as fluffy blankets, comforters, pillows, or toys
- No drop sides
- Metal hardware and springs

The Car Seat

Though it technically goes in your car and not in your house, you'll need to get a car seat right away so you can transport your wild infant from the hospital to her new habitat. (Unless, of course, you live in your car—in that case, you can just call your car seat a "seat." But really, your first step should be to find a non-Chevrolet type of dwelling for you and baby Jewel to live in.)

Because car seats have rapidly evolved over the years, it is important to make sure yours is up to date and super safe. The most current car seats are rear facing, and include tether straps that attach to anchors behind the seats in your car. (These anchors are installed in all new cars since the model year 2001.) Sadly, you won't be able to tether or anchor your child during her teen years.

You can choose between an infant-specific car seat or one that will work from infancy through toddlerhood—there are a mind-blowing number of choices out there. There are even booster seats designed for kids up to age twelve. Yes, that twelve-year-old is probably going to resent you. Visit *www.nhtsa .gov* for a thorough rundown of your options.

BLANKET SAFETY

If you use a blanket to keep your baby warm at night (instead of a sleeper or sleepsack, which doctors usually recommend), tuck it under the mattress so that it only covers your infant up to her chest. Then put your infant to sleep with her feet near the end that has the blanket tucked under it. This is to ensure that the blanket can't cover your infant's face.

FIND A PEDIATRICIAN

Believe it or not, you need to find your wild infant a doctor before she makes her exit into the real world. That's so once she arrives, you've got someone ready and able to handle any old Coxsackie, cradle cap, or reflux that infant might lob his or her way.

Find a good pediatrician you can trust. You will want someone who is well qualified, is a good listener, and is covered by your health insurance. Also, you want someone who doesn't mind you calling at all hours and freaking out over every little thing. Trust me. Perhaps the best way to find a pediatrician is to ask other parents in your area who they'd recommend. You can work this into the conversation where you're begging them to divulge to you the secret of sweet, sweet, elusive sleep.

You should also make sure that the hospital where your doctor has privileges is covered by your insurance. Having your child treated at an out-of-network hospital can get very pricey.

GENERAL BABYPROOFING

Before bringing a wild infant into your home, it is essential that you prepare an appropriate and safe nesting area for your young. After all, she will actively seek out any available trouble just like a heat-seeking missile seeks . . . things that are hot, I guess (chicken soup? Jake Gyllenhaal?).

Anyway, wild infants seek trouble. They don't necessarily mean it—they actually have no idea what trouble is. They just do whatever they want all the time, and trouble is what tends to result. That's why you need to anticipate said trouble and avoid it at all costs. Luckily, many smart wildlife professionals have already determined what's safe for your nest.

REMEMBER:
EVERY INFANT'S AN INDIVIDUAL!

Every wild infant has her own idea of what sort of calamitous trouble would be the most fun, and some of them can be really creative. So observe your tiny creature. Does she seem to think reaching into the toilet is an awesome idea? Does the idea of taking down the Christmas tree and eating glass ornaments and pine needles put a glimmer in her eye? Keep track of what she fixates on, and childproof accordingly.

The *Kingdomius infantius* native requires very specific nesting conditions in order to thrive in captivity. There should be no harmful materials, irritants, or cigarette-smoking humans in the enclosure. This is so the wild infant does not harm himself or others, have a massive attack of fussiness, or become a jaded little secondhand smoker before he can even talk (next thing you know, he'll be asking for a dry martini). The newly domesticated wild infant has no idea how to protect himself—he doesn't even know which parts of his body belong to him, and which are potential food (he'll probably try to gnaw off his own feet later, but you don't have to worry about that just yet).

Basically, the job of preventing harm to your wild infant falls entirely to you at this point. Therefore, you must set up your domicile with this crazy little human in mind. Here are some key areas to check.

Hot Water Heater Temperature

Young *Kingdomius infantius* specimens are very sensitive to hot water. Remember, their skin is brand new and has not yet become leathery from sun, hard work, and cruel, cruel time the way yours probably has. What's more, the little gals and fellas do not have the quick reflexes needed to move away from scalding water and prevent burns. So, what does this mean for you? For one thing, you should never, ever listen to a baby when they try to weasel their way into the Jacuzzi with you. They're totally full of it. In addition, it means you should lower your hot water heater's maximum temperature to 120°F before you bring your wild infant home. To be sure, test the water temperature with a cooking thermometer. If you are unsure of how to do this, call the electric company or the maker of the hot water heater.

Is the Air Clean?

Secondhand smoke is a serious threat to your fragile young *Kingdomius infantius* offspring. Not only does it have the potential to make him act like a cynical advertising executive from the 1950s; it also increases his risk of ear infections, allergies, and asthma. Babies whose parents smoke also have a greater risk of Sudden Infant Death Syndrome (SIDS). This is true whether the smoking is done out in the wilderness or in the home habitat. So if you were thinking, "Oh, I'll just smoke outside!" you can think again. Close, but no cigar (see how I did that?). If you need help quitting, and you know you do, talk to your doctor or go to a website like *www.quitsmoking.about.com.*

Install Detectors

Many of the most dangerous threats to the wild infant—other than his own teeth, once they come in—are actually invisible. Stealthy predators such as carbon monoxide gas and lead can be very hazardous, and unfortunately, you can't shoot them with a tranquilizer gun and have them taken to the zoo (no one wants to pay for tickets to go see carbon monoxide!). Instead, you need to take steps to detect and eradicate them from your ecosystem.

When you install smoke detectors in your home (and you definitely should), you might want to consider carbon monoxide detectors as well. These should be installed near your bedrooms and on all floors of your dwelling.

See if You Have Lead

Lead is another potential danger that should be banished from your ecosystem. It can be a very sneaky predator, and may appear in various forms and in many hiding places.

Paint

The biggest source of lead is paint in older homes. If your dwelling was built before 1950, be on the lookout for peeling, chipping paint. Your wild baby has no idea that paint chips are not awesome to eat (no, not even with honey mustard sauce) so you will have to persuade him otherwise.

The only effective way to get rid of lead paint is to have a trained professional remove it for you and provide a certification that it was done safely and completely. Then you and your family can have a party to celebrate! Just make sure you don't decorate with lead balloons—I hear they're not so festive, anyway.

Water

Lead can also rear its ugly head in drinking water. Lead gets into drinking water through the use of lead pipes. No, not the lead pipes used by Professor Plum or Miss Scarlet in Clue. But come to think of it, you don't want that kind of lead pipe around your baby, either. Especially not in the billiard room!

Although lead pipes usually only exist in homes built before 1930, some newer homes might have been connected with lead solder (no, I am not sure what that is, either, but I'm sure it's not good). Also, pipes can be made with up to 8 percent lead and still be called "lead-free." And you don't want your wild infant to be 92 percent free, 8 percent leaden, do you?

Here are some tips for protecting your little creature from lead in your drinking water:

🐾 **Go for the cold**—If you think your plumbing might have lead in it, use only cold water from the tap to make formula, or for cooking or drinking. This is because hot water can have higher levels of lead than cold water. Whether or not you decide to take cold showers is entirely your business!

🐾 **Let it flow**—Let your water run for about fifteen to thirty seconds before you use it, to flush the lead out of the pipes. You can do that trick where you let it run for the amount of time it takes to sing "Happy Birthday," or something. After a while, your wild infant might become annoyed with this false alarm, and wonder where the hell her birthday present is. Just tell her, "Your present is lead-free water." This will work exactly one time—if that.

❧ **Filter up**—You might also consider a water filter for reducing the amount of lead in your drinking water. This might help prevent that whole "Happy Birthday" debacle and all the tears and disappointment left in its wake.

If you are worried that your wild infant may have been exposed to lead, talk to your pediatrician about having him tested.

Lead in the Workplace

If you (or your adult human partner) repair cars or radiators, make stained glass or pottery, or work in construction or welding—or get shot with lead bullets often—you should be sure to wash and change your clothing and shoes prior to leaving your foraging site.

Top Ten Household Dangers

Obviously, your wild infant is the single most dangerous thing in your home, but these are the things he can do the most damage with. Drumroll, please.

10. Poisonous plants (yum!)

9. Venetian blind cords (whee!)

8. Electrical cords (zap!)

7. Electrical outlets (a.k.a. "insert fork here")

6. Stoves, heaters, and hot appliances

5. Toxic household products

4. Medicine

3. Water (isn't there a saying about babies and bathwater?)

2. Coins or other small objects

1. Stairs

JUNGLE
PLAYDATE

Mother alligators aren't exactly warm and fuzzy, but they show some amazing planning skills and dedication when it comes to their little gator babies. Mama makes nests of rotting organic matter (awww!) that are self-incubating and help nurture the eggs. Yeah, rotting organic matter might not be your number one choice in crib material, but this stuff is actually designed to determine the gender of the babies. What do you have to say now, gator haters? Apparently nests that are made with leaves equal more boy gator infants than those made with wet marsh. Once this control-freak mom has genetically engineered her offspring and the eggs hatch, she protects her kids by carrying them in her mouth. Imagine the temptation—she's an alligator, for God's sake! (Baby shower hint: Do not give a mom alligator Baby Crocs as a gift. She won't be amused.)

— —

Chapter 2

ENCOUNTERING THE WILD INFANT

Once you have prepared your domicile for the arrival of the wild creature, the next step is the careful trapping and relocation of the feral *Kingdomius infantius* specimen from the creature's native habitat in the womb. Such a delicate transport is usually best handled by a trained infant wildlife expert (obstetrician). These experts know the best techniques for coaxing the wild infant out into the open.

THE GLORIOUS MEET-N-GREET

You will most likely encounter your *Kingdomius infantius* for the first time in the hospital. Be prepared for this initial meeting to be breathtaking, but also somewhat awkward. For one thing, the infant won't even have the good manners to say "Hi." For another thing, unless your wild baby was born via C-section, she most likely is going to look like a slimy, profoundly unhappy raisin with hair.

Don't be alarmed, and most of all, do not run away screaming. Not only is that distracting to the hospital staff; it is pointless. Instead, make a grand gesture of holding up your infant for all passersby to see, preferably accompanied by an Elton John ballad. Why? Because (a) Elton John music will soothe your panic, and (b) the wild infant's unfortunate face will be above your eye level and pointed away from you. Don't even try to tell me that's not what that scene was all about in *The Lion King*!

WHAT HAPPENS NEXT

During those first few days in the hospital, you'll be surrounded by zoologists who know exactly what to do in any situation. Take advantage of their expertise to "learn" and "observe your wild infant up close in a secure environment"—in other words, sleep. Sure, you have to feed the child, and hold it for the requisite photos . . . but in general, you've got *lots* of backup. So sleep! And also, try to eat, although eating hospital food is the equivalent of foraging desperately for food in the forest (and finding nothing but an old tire and some mud-encrusted Silly String). Bon appétit!

Here are some of the things that will happen while you're drooling on the hospital pillow.

Apgar Score

Your wild infant will barely have entered the world before she is put through a battery of scientific tests. The first of these is the Apgar, which is an evaluation of your baby's physical condition. This is given at one minute and five minutes after birth (not even enough time for the poor thing to fix her hair!). This test measures her heart rate, breathing, responsiveness, muscle tone, and appearance.

Few babies score a perfect 10 on the Apgar test (who does this Apgar chick think she is to go around judging babies, anyway?), so you might not want to hurt your baby's feelings by announcing her score in your Facebook status. Anyway, I heard that Angelina Jolie was a total Apgar 2, and look how she turned out!

. . . And More Tests

The Apgar test is just the beginning of the endless string of tests your untamed baby must endure before she goes home to you. No wonder she's cranky!

At some point, someone is going to prick your infant's heel to test for phenylketonuria (PKU), hypothyroidism, and other disorders. Your wild baby might also be given an infant hearing test, to determine just how well she will be able to ignore you when you beg her to stop screeching.

Medicines and Vaccines

Since untamed *Kingdomius infantius* specimens are totally feral and germy, they might need some medicines and vaccinations right away. For example, they might need antibiotic drops or ointments in their eyes to prevent infections from bacteria or exposure to sexually transmitted diseases. (Do you really want to know? Didn't think so.) The American Academy of Pediatrics recommends a shot of vitamin K for all babies in case of deficiency. Not to be outdone, the Centers for Disease Control recommends that babies be given their first hepatatis B vaccine at birth.

Basically, your poor infant will be given so many needles, she'll feel like a little voodoo doll. That explains why she'll flinch the second you try to change her diaper.

HOW TO HOLD A WILD INFANT

You may have been told, or will be told, that you will "just know" what to do once your wild infant has emerged from its enclosure and has been relocated to your habitat. This is like saying you should "just know" how to handle an angry rattlesnake if it were placed in your lap (hint: screaming your head off and begging for anti-venom is not the proper response).

The truth is, if you've only ever held the wild infants of friends or family members, and you have done so awkwardly and nervously, you're probably not going to feel comfortable immediately. Now that the untamed, wriggling creature is "yours," you might feel just as nervous and awkward, in addition to being totally responsible for his survival.

Avoid that sense of cluelessness by reading up on some of the most common ways to hold a wild infant, according to *www .TheLaborofLove.com*:

The Cradle/Rock Hold

This is probably the best basic way for beginners to hold a wild infant. It's so simple, it only has one step:

1. **Place the baby's head securely in the crook of one of your arms and wrap your other arm around the untamed infant.**

Keep in mind that an untamed infant's head is often the wildest part of his body; he has very poor control of his head at this point. So make sure you support his head well, and don't allow it to loll around. Wild infants find this hold to be very soothing, and may fall into a comfortable sleep. They may also spit up on your face, but you must continue to support the head even as it spews vomit onto you.

The Shoulder/Upright Hold

This is a little bit fancier, and might be good to try after you have mastered the Cradle/Rock Hold.

1. **Lean the wild infant up against one of your shoulders, and wrap the arm of the same side around the infant's butt.**

2. **Use your other arm to support the infant's back and/or neck.**

Many untamed babies can sleep in this position, too. Watch and see what your wild infant prefers; perhaps he thinks it's a bit soon for you to be touching his butt. Respect his wishes.

The Belly Hold

This position is supposed to be great for babies with colic or gas, which we will discuss later on.

1. **Lay the wild infant chest down over one of your forearms, with his head in your hand. (You can also do this across your lap.)**

2. **Lay your other arm across the infant's back to hold him securely.**

This position puts pressure on the wild infant's belly, and may provide relief from gas pain.

Is He Cute Yet?

You might still be cringing at the rather disturbing appearance of this wild creature you have brought into existence. Truly, this can be a frightening thing to witness, even once the infant has been de-slimed. Keep in mind that the journey out of the womb through the birth canal is a rather harrowing one. If you are the adult human female, it's a little bit your fault for having such an ergonomically flawed canal. Luckily, the infant will not need to travel that route ever again.

Here are some of the alarming physical characteristics your infant may possess:

- Head molding—This takes the form of a misshapen or pointy "cone" head, which is the result of being squeezed coming through the birth canal. This might take a week or even longer to resolve itself. In the meantime, try to think of all of the awesome things that come in cone shapes: snowcones, party hats, Madonna's boobs. Also, this is a good time to break out one of those adorable hats someone gave you as a baby gift. For example, you could try one of those hats with puppy-dog ears—most people will assume your infant is a triangle-headed shar-pei. Or lamb ears! Awww! Mary had a little lamb with a trilateral skull!

- A caput—This is another charming head feature, characterized by fluid squeezed into your infant's head. It basically looks like a bump or swollen section on the head, and will only add to the cone look. This, too, will go away on its own.

- Swollen eyelids—Again, the journey out of utero is exhausting. You and your adult human partner probably have these, too, so let's not judge.

- Flattened nose—Yes, her nose will probably look like it's been hit repeatedly with a frying pan *Looney Tunes* style. This is due to pressure from that ridiculously narrow birth canal of yours.

- Floppy ears—Sadly, the ear cartilage wasn't quite finished when your wild infant came out. The cartilage will harden in the next few months, so until then, don't go getting your infant's floppy ears pinned.

- Fine body hair—And I don't mean "fine" in a good way. I mean "fine" in a "less thick than Teen Wolf's but still covering his entire body" way.

- Swollen labia, scrotum, or breasts—This is just weird, and is caused by prebirth maternal hormones. Yet another possible explanation for your wild infant's crankiness—maybe it's PMS!

- 🐾 Peeling skin—I know what you're thinking: This skin is brand new, why should it be peeling? It just does.
- 🐾 Bluish hands or feet—Attention: This circulatory system isn't 100 percent up and running yet. Please pardon our appearance!
- 🐾 Reddish-purplish skin—All wild infants are born with reddish-purplish skin, which then turns to pinkish-red. Oh, and at some point it might be yellow, too.
- 🐾 Bow legs—This situation is caused by being scrunched up in the uterus for nine months. It usually goes away, but if not, your infant will look like an adorable old man forever (that's still an improvement on the current situation)!

Despite these, ahem, imperfections, your wild infant will certainly have *some* delightfully cute bodily features you can focus on and photograph ad nauseam. Look at those little fingernails, for example! My advice is to focus on the cute stuff while the not-so-attractive stuff resolves itself. P.S.: There is absolutely nothing wrong with sending people baby pictures of fingernails only—don't let anyone tell you otherwise!

About Jaundice

One condition your wild infant might encounter postbirth is jaundice. You may have already heard about jaundice, which is a condition caused by increased amounts of a pigment called bilirubin. Bilirubin is produced by the normal breakdown of red blood cells, and too much of it causes the skin to have a yellowish tinge. This, ladies and gentlemen, is jaundice. It is pleased to meet you.

Perhaps because it occurs in both boys and girls, jaundice has the good sense to appear in a tasteful, gender-neutral yellow.

"Standard" Jaundice

"Normal" jaundice appears in about half of all babies within the first few days of life, and usually goes away in a week or two. Your wild infant usually poops out the excess bilirubin during that time.

Something known as "breastmilk jaundice" is a bit less common, although it looks the same. This type usually happens between days four and seven and can last three to ten weeks. One great way to flush this out is to nurse more frequently, every one and a half to two hours during the day and at least every four hours at night. This will encourage frequent pooping by your wild infant.

Jaundice That Needs Treating

Jaundice usually resolves itself, but there are some cases where the hospital staff will take some action, or, if you're already home, you will need to call the pediatrician. If your baby becomes dehydrated or feverish, the pediatrician definitely needs to take a look. Likewise, call the doctor if he's deep yellow or orange, has fewer than three bowel movements per day, or still looks yellow after two weeks.

If your wild baby's bilirubin levels go too high, the doctor might want to have your baby go "under the lights." No, these are not McDonald's-type burger warmers, but special lights designed to break up bilirubin. The bilirubin is then pooped out by the wild infant.

BRINGING THE WILD INFANT HOME

After some time spent observing your untamed infant from a comfortable distance in the hospital, it is time to transport your young back to your nest. This will definitely feel strange. It's not often that you and your partner leave the house as two people, then come home as three because another human fell out of one of your bodies. You might also find that you are alarmed by every little stop sign and bump in the road as you transport your vulnerable little newborn home in your safari vehicle. He's so fragile! Plus, the fact that his head so closely resembles a traffic cone just naturally reminds you to drive more cautiously.

Early Domestication

The first week or so at home will be a time for you to examine and become acquainted with the wild creature as it gets used to your ecosystem. Observing the behaviors of the wild infant in his new habitat is very interesting. Use binoculars for wild infant watching at your own risk; expect the binoculars to be peed or vomited on. You may take field notes, but likewise expect these to become soiled.

Here are some tips for surviving this adjustment period.

Take Some "Vacation" Time

If you can manage it, it is often very helpful for both the male and female specimen of your household to take time off from work when the wild creature is first brought home. This is not only for the purposes of observing the offspring and his strange ways, but also to assist in nesting with your young.

Sometimes, the female human in particular exhibits discomfort, exhaustion, and odd crying jags during this initial transition. These behaviors may or may not occur while the female devours chocolate-covered sea salt and bleeds. All of this is normal, but is best not observed by one's coworkers.

The male, on the other hand, has to adjust to his once-familiar female mate now taking on a new role, and the all-new character of the wild infant. You will find that observing the female in her new role is almost as fascinating as observing the squirmy creature she has birthed. However, if you are a male staying home to observe the safari in your home, simply nodding and saying,

"Hmm, how fascinating!" may place your life at risk. You must actively assist the female in the various feeding and grooming rituals, or she might just string you up by a "crotch dangler" carrier tailor-made for you. Bye-bye, manhood!

Seek Assistance

As you embark on your earliest baby-watching adventures, you should accept help whenever it is offered. Well, perhaps not from an escaped psychiatric patient or a Scientologist (or a combination of the two). But if a trusted friend—especially one who has already domesticated a wild infant!—or family member offers assistance, you should jump on it. Parents and in-laws are an annoying breed by nature, but most of them do have prior experience with the wild *Kingdomius infantius* species.

When allowing members of your tribe to assist you, make sure you tell them exactly what you need them to do. If you need help with the mountain of regurgitated-milk laundry and they give you sixteen varieties of tiered fruitcake, you are not making the best use of their potential.

Establish Visiting Hours

It's helpful to institute visiting hours, so you can control when crowds come to view and photograph the wild animal. Encourage groups visiting your home safari to avoid alarming the wild infant through flash photography or loud comments. Also, encourage them to use red-eye reduction when taking pictures, so your wild infant won't come out looking like a laboratory rat. Most importantly, be sure to close your safari to the public at a certain hour. Assure everyone that you will be open again tomorrow, and that they can feel free to take a "souvenir" of wild infant laundry home with them.

Sleep/Rest

As previously mentioned, many of your most basic physical needs will now be met (or not met) at the whim of your unpredictable wild infant. In particular, the small squirmy one will have frighteningly unchecked power in dictating your sleep habits, at least for a while. And when your wild infant says you may sleep, *sleep*!

"But how will I know when my wild infant is giving me permission to sleep and/or nap?" you might ask. Good question! The answer is really simple: you sleep when the baby sleeps. The permission to sleep is implied by the fact that the infant is unconscious and unable to argue about it. Be aware that this sleep will probably be snatched in nonconsecutive, random chunks. To which I say, who cares? It's sleep! Leave those dishes for now, and take advantage!

Unplug

During the first stages of studying your wild infant, interruptions from other well-intended humans can seriously impede your fact-finding mission. While it may be tempting to pick up the telephone and say, "Hi" or "For the love of God, please help me!" to a friend or acquaintance, this can get in the way of bonding with your untamed baby. Remember, there is much to learn about his uncoordinated, loud, and leaky ways, so resist the temptation to be "saved by the bell." Set your outgoing voicemail or answering machine to a birth announcement, and unplug the phone. (Keep a cell phone charged just in case your wild infant tries to devour you whole.)

Pets and Your Wild Infant

It is possible that, prior to bringing home this strange creature we call the *Kingdomius infantius* specimen, you've already been sharing your home with a semi-domesticated species of animal. This might be a dog (*Canis lupus familiaris*), a cat (*Felis catus*), or perhaps a hamster (*Mesocricetus auratus*). Here is some basic information about introducing the wild infant to these critters:

- If your semi-domesticated animal companion happens to be a hamster, you're in luck. Hamsters are rather dull-witted and emotionally detached, and really won't give one hoot about the arrival of your wild infant, as long as they are still receiving a reasonable portion of hamster pellets and water. Really, your hamster doesn't even care about you; he doesn't know who the hell you are. He just runs on that annoying wheel all day long. Why do you even have this hamster, anyway?

- If your pet creature is a dog, it'll be something of a mixed bag. Dogs can be rather needy for attention from their human companions, and might notice a decline in said attention once a wild infant enters the home. On the plus side, however, wild infants will eventually spill food that a dog can lap up. Hmm . . . attention vs. food, attention vs. food . . . wait, is that a glob of something possibly edible? Food wins! Dog hearts infant.

- A cat probably won't be as crushed by a rival for attention, as long as she still is able to do her two favorite things: sleep and be worshiped. Just continue to pay adoring tribute to your lovely feline on a regular basis, and she will continue to allow you to provide her with gourmet food and a satin cat bed. Carry on, if you must!

Tips for Helping a Pet to Adjust

Here are some other tips for a safe and happy pet/baby wildlife integration.

- Make sure your pet has her vaccinations up to date and her nails are trimmed.

- Try to resolve any pet behavioral issues (jumping, nipping, etc.) before you bring the wild infant into your home. This is much easier than trying to address those problems once your wild infant is on the premises, disrupting your sleep and causing mayhem with her own behavioral issues.

- ❧ If your untamed young's room will be off-limits to your pet, install a gate prior to bringing the wild infant home. Be consistent in training your pet not to enter the room.

- ❧ When you are holding the writhing, gurgling little creature, allow your pet to sniff her and become accustomed to her strange musk. Reward your pet with treats for appropriate behavior. If you're more comfortable, you can also gradually introduce your pet to the infant's smell by letting the pet sniff a piece of the baby's clothing. Don't let your pet eat the baby's clothing—that would be starting things off on the wrong foot, don't you think?

- ❧ As your untamed offspring grows, teach her how to play with your family pet in a safe and appropriate way. This type of play will *not* come naturally to the infant, since she is basically a wild little hooligan with no impulse control. Encourage gentle and careful interactions.

- ❧ If your pet shows signs of aggression, talk to your veterinarian immediately about techniques to handle this problem.

Keeping Baby Safe at Home

In the beginning, your wild infant is more or less a squirmy little blob who probably thinks dangerous thoughts, but cannot yet act on them. Or maybe he doesn't even think. Still, there are some things to be on the lookout for, even at this early stage. Even though you've already done your best to babyproof your nest, your wild infant will somehow still find hazards that leave you in a constant state of worry and panic. Here are some of the wild dangers your infant may encounter even within the sheltered environment of your domicile.

Falls

Before your untamed infant is able to move about, you'd think you could put him down in a safe place and expect him to stay there. However, they are so squirmy and spastic that they can often move more than you think, even very early on. And, needless to say, once he develops the skill of rolling around, all bets are off. Infants usually start to roll over between two and six months of age, and once they start rolling, they generally keep on rolling.

As an overall rule of thumb, once a wild infant acquires a new skill, he won't just do it once; he'll practice the shit out of it. It's not like how it is for us grown adult humans, who, say, take one yoga or interior design class and never go back. No, wild infants learn this stuff, and then they focus on it like it's their job— because it is. So, the dude's gonna roll. A lot. And remember that whole fire safety drill, "Stop, Drop, and Roll?" Unfortunately, the wild infant tends to confuse the order of those instructions.

The bottom line: You shouldn't wait until your infant rolls over for the first time to start taking preventative action. Start now. It's pretty simple: don't leave the wild infant alone on a bed, changing table, or anything he could roll off of.

PLAYDATE

The Japanese Cardinal Fish starts out trying to be a good dad, but he seriously drops the ball. By "the ball," I mean "his babies," and by "drops," I mean "eats." He's a type of fish that's called a "mouth brooder," which means he incubates his kids in his mouth until they're ready to be released into the ocean. Mrs. Cardinal Fish is like, "Look, can I trust you with this? It's kind of super-important." And he's like, "God, will you quit nagging already? Who can't incubate babies in their mouth? I've got it under control."

It's all well and good, until he sees another good-looking female. He thinks, "Man, I wish I wasn't such a dorky minivan mouth brooder." Then he proceeds to eat his kids and swims off with his new lady. Who, by the way, lets him stow her kids in his mouth, too.

- -

Choking

Because the wild infant subsists more or less on a liquid diet for his first months of life, there isn't much concern that he will choke on any solid foods. However, there's a twist—and it's that damn rolling over again. Rolling over puts your wild infant in a position to get his little mitts on some choking hazards and pop them into his mouth. Such hazards include small pieces of hard candy, coins, small magnets, buttons, marbles, and any other small items he might encounter during a rollover session. Be sure to keep these objects out of your infant's reach at all times, and heed the anti-rollover advice above. In the meantime, be sure you are trained in current methods of infant first aid if your baby chokes.

SIDS

Sudden Infant Death Syndrome, or SIDS, is a serious risk to wild infants, and one you are probably familiar with. You may already know that you can protect your untamed infant from this danger by making sure he sleeps on his back rather than his stomach. In addition to this, there are other steps you can take to reduce your baby's risk of SIDS.

- 🐾 To be safest, avoid side sleeping. This is definitely better than letting your infant sleep on his stomach, but not as safe as sleeping on his back. Side sleepers may—yes, you guessed it—roll over onto their stomachs.
- 🐾 Make sure to instruct all caregivers to put your infant to sleep on his back.
- 🐾 Don't let your infant get overheated while sleeping.
- 🐾 Avoid lining your baby's crib with bumper pads.
- 🐾 Do not allow anyone to smoke around your infant.

Chapter 3

THE WILD INFANT AT REST

Your wild infant definitely likes to sleep. A lot. The only thing she seems to enjoy more than sleeping is making sure you don't sleep. It's a tough job, but someone has to do it, right?

SLEEP PATTERNS EXPLAINED

Even though the untamed *Kingdomius infantius* specimen can sleep an average of fifteen hours a day at first, these hours are often chosen randomly, not at all consecutively, and largely during daylight hours. Basically, this wild child of yours likes to mix it up, keep it interesting. And by "interesting," I mean totally hellish and exhausting.

See, when the wild infant existed in the prenatal environment, she was actually rocked to sleep by your moving around during the day. So, what for you was "going to work" or "doing really strenuous prenatal yoga" or "carrying slabs of cinderblock up a ladder" was just one soothing, long lullaby for her.

Conversely, when you stopped moving at night, her first thought was, "Party time!" She danced all night; she practiced taekwondo; she maybe crank-called your spleen just for the hell of it.

Helping Your Infant Understand Day and Night

Now that she's in the new habitat of your home, she sees no reason to alter her rock 'n' roll lifestyle. Oh, but you do. You really, really do.

It's up to you to teach your wild creature that as far as living it up goes, daytime is totally where it's at. Here are some suggestions.

Give Her Daytime Wakeup Calls

One approach is to wake your wild infant up every two hours during the day. At first you might feel like a bit of a jerk for doing this, but after she's kept you awake at night for a solid month or so, you will begin to take a sadistic, sleep-deprived delight in watching that little face crumple up in puzzled annoyance. *Yeah, you see how that feels?* you'll think, as that sweet little prune face starts to fuss at the indignity of being woken up before she was ready. *Come on, give me ten jumping jacks! Oh, right, you can't even sit up. Never mind.*

When you do wake her up, make it fun for her. Bring out the fun baby toys, play peekaboo, carry her outside to listen to the birds. This way, you are sending the message, "Daytime rocks!" Sure, it's kind of a lie, but babies are really gullible.

Emphasize: Night Is Boring!

At nighttime, reverse your untamed infant's nocturnal nature by making things boring. Refuse to play with her, keep the lighting dim, and totally ignore her "R U awake?" text messages. Don't even change her diaper unless the thing has become its own frightening ecosystem. By the time she's been in her new habitat for six to twelve weeks, she should be starting to sleep for five to six hours at night. She might also start taking two or three one- to two-hour naps during the day.

Establish a Nap Schedule

Once your wild infant begins to take naps, you should try to regulate these naps to encourage nighttime sleep. For example, a *Kingdomius infantius* specimen who parties all afternoon and naps at 5 P.M. will likely awaken at bedtime, ready for another wild infant party. For this reason, you should use all of your best boredom tactics to encourage napping as early in the afternoon as possible. Read her your income tax filings if necessary.

GETTING BABY TO SLEEP

Inevitably, your baby will fall asleep when you do not want him to, then insist on staying awake when he should really be sleeping. It's like that old saying, "Late to bed, every fifteen minutes to rise, makes mom hallucinate and bleed from her eyes." Wait—that's not the saying at all, is it?

Anyway, the more sleep-deprived you are, the more you will begin to feel as though each night, you are preparing yourself for a showdown with the most tough-as-nails adversary you have ever encountered. The little creature has a flinty will, lungs that won't quit, and a youthful energy that you will never, ever have again. He can go all night. And he will.

What do you have on your side? Well, a fully developed brain, for one thing, although you have probably lost a few cells recently. Still, though, you can use your sophisticated manipulation techniques to trick that little sucker to sleep.

The Drop-and-Go

One proven trick to lull the untamed baby into a sizable nap is to let her fall asleep in your arms, then gently place her down on her back in the crib. Keep one hand on her chest the whole time, and once she's lying down, place both hands on her for a minute or so, and then lift them slowly. This little magic trick doesn't work for all wild infants (some seem to sense immediately when they're in a ten-foot radius of their crib), but it seems to work often enough to justify giving it a try. **Note**: The "laying on of hands" will not faith-heal your infant.

Hands-Free Rocking

As we've mentioned before, movement is a time-tested strategy for World War Zzzzz. By gently moving the wild *Kingdomius infantius* specimen, you will cause their womb-friendly "sleepy-time" mechanism to kick in. (**Note**: Casting your baby off to sea on an ice floe, putting him on a train to Looneyville, Texas, or forcing him to do Pilates are all sources of motion, but are seriously frowned upon and probably illegal.)

Sometimes, though, you might think you need your sore, exhausted arms and hands free to, say, weave a basket, stalk your ex on Facebook, or do a version of "Itsy Bitsy Spider" in which the spider goes postal and eats the entire town. At these times, try out products that can gently rock your baby so you can pursue whatever insane tasks you mistakenly think are valid. Products such as a vibrating bouncy seat or a wind-up swing are great for this.

Sing Lullabies

A playlist of soothing, sleep-inducing songs is another possible way to convince your wild infant that it is time to sleep. Certainly any Celine Dion song ought to do the trick, and classic lullaby songs are great, too. You can also use background noise of stuff like waves and seagulls, but be warned that down the road, your child might end up feeling affection for those nasty rats with wings. Eww!

Hit the Road

If you are dangerously sleep-deprived, do *not* try this one at home—or not at home. If you feel fairly lucid, though, you can take your wild infant for a drive. An automobile ride combines the best of gentle rocking motion, a humming engine sound, and soothing bumps in the road. **Note**: Do *not* drive your wild infant really far away and then leave him somewhere. You *will* face charges, and besides, he'll probably find his way back, and be really, really angry.

Get Him Attached to a Lovey

Many zoologists and scientists say that the wild infant can be persuaded to bond with a "lovey" or a "transitional object" such as a stuffed animal. Once this bond with the lovey has been established, the child will reach for this item when he wants to be calmed down. By giving him the lovey, you can help the wild infant to be mollified into sleep. Many wild infants continue to utilize these "transitional objects" even in adulthood, although at that point, they are called "one-night stands." Aww!

SLEEP DEPRIVATION: HANDLING YOUR OWN WILD BEHAVIORS

After enduring a certain amount of sleep deprivation imposed by your untamed little creature, you may find yourself (or your partner) behaving in a rather beastly manner as well. Zoologists have observed that after a sustained state of sleep deprivation, the adult human displays dramatic behavior changes and greatly decreased mental capacity. You might be forgetful, disorganized, and ridiculously emotional.

You might find yourself attempting to have a debate with the static on the baby monitor, and then begin to think that the static really does make a lot of good sense. You might notice silent tears are streaming down your cheeks as you sing the *Bob the Builder* theme song ("Can We Fix It?") before replying, "No, no, I'm afraid we can't."

Or maybe it is your partner who is exhibiting these chilling behaviors. Either way, the individual who is behaving in this fashion has become a temporarily feral creature, and may act out in any number of ways. For this reason, the adult human in most dire need must be permitted to sleep, for the well-being of your entire household.

Following are tips for ensuring a balance of sanity for the adult members of your tribe.

Share the Night Feedings

If your baby can drink from a bottle and you feel that you are on the brink of sleep-deprived insanity, ask the adult male in your home to feed your young from time to time. The adult male might complain, "But I need to wake up for work in the morning." This may be true, but you need to get up and not go off the deep end while trying to raise this crazy little mammal. Yes, it's a bit of a lose-lose situation for a while, but it won't last forever!

Add a Feeding During the Day

Maybe your wild infant had been sleeping fairly well during the night, but then started waking up all greedy for more food. One approach to decreasing the nighttime wakeups is to add a feeding during the day. This will keep the wild infant in a sleepy milk-coma.

Avoid Sleep Envy

You might encounter other humans who will love to tell you how their untamed baby sleeps "like a baby" (in other words, not at all like a baby) through the night. You must not compare yourself to these specimens, as it will only get you down. To begin with, most adult humans who make this claim are totally full of meconium (you'll learn about this later), and others are spinning the truth to sound better than it is. The rest are just plain lucky, and that's all the more reason you should not compare yourself.

For a while, your baby's sleep schedule will just be part of her natural rhythms. Eventually, you can get in there and reprogram it. Before you know it, you will be telling this untamed youth when to sleep and she will have to obey. In the meantime, know you're not alone—millions of other *Maternicus martyrius* and their partners are in the same boat as you.

Jungle PLAYDATE

The giant Pacific octopus might not be the cutest animal, but she is the most selfless mom in the world. Because octopus eggs are full of protein and as delicious as caviar to ocean predators, this mom stands guard over them and protects them with her life. After laying up to 100,000 eggs, she stays in her den with them, never leaving them for a moment. I mean, she doesn't even leave to go get herself some quick takeout food. She does this for six or seven months until the babies hatch. Of course, not eating for six or seven months does take its toll, and she soon dies. Which is really sad, because with her eight arms, she'd surely be the best multitasking mom ever.

- -

SLEEP TRAINING METHODS

For some adult humans, observing your wild infant's sleep habits and attempting to gradually normalize him is not quite enough. No, you need a trendy parenting technique, something superprogressive, maybe a little controversial, and definitely debated on Internet discussion boards. For you folks, wait no longer! Here are some exciting methods to argue about with your friends. Arguing really helps as far as staying awake, BTW.

Ferberizing

"Ferberizing" might sound like some iffy new food-processing technique, but it's actually a time-tested wild infant sleep method. The process involves putting the wild infant into his nesting area (crib or bassinet) and checking on the baby when he begins to scream bloody murder. The key is to not pick the infant up, feed him, or give him anything at all that he might want; simply reassure him, stretch out the time between your check-ins, and cut back on the visits with each passing night. It's hard to tell when a baby has become fully Ferberized; some might cry when a companion leaves their bedroom well into their forties.

American Academy of Pediatrics Method

The AAP recommends establishing very specific prebedtime rituals for the wild infant, such as a bath or storybook, so he will come to associate these activities with imminent sleep. The adult specimen can also dim the lights, quiet things down, and offer the baby a lovey, if that works. If the untamed baby wakes up at some point during the night, don't rush in there right away. Let the lovey do its job. (**Note**: Used-up old loveys often become bitter, cynical, and sarcastic in their retirement years. Would it hurt for you to pay for Lovey's therapy? Just saying.)

Dr. Sears and the Family Bed

Many years ago, the wild infant and his mature human parents slept together in the same nest, mostly because there wasn't really room in the house for them to sleep anywhere else. In more recent history, this approach got a makeover and some sensitivity training, and became "cosleeping," a key aspect of "attachment parenting." This philosophy says that it's more important for an infant to feel secure and bonded than to develop independent sleeping habits.

One awesome thing about having the untamed infant right next to you is that you can breastfeed him without fully waking up yourself. On the minus side, OMG, you could smush your baby! No, really—there was a warning issued and everything. Dr. Sears himself even recommends an Arm's Reach Co-Sleeper Bassinet now.

Dr. Weissbluth's Sleep Training

Dr. Marc Weissbluth, the author of *Healthy Sleep Habits, Happy Child*, is a sleep disorder specialist, and this totally makes sense, since infancy is a sleep disorder. Dr. Weissbluth maintains that consistent naptimes and early bedtimes are the key to your wild specimen's slumber. He said an untamed infant who is "too tired" won't be able to sleep (this is rarely an issue for you these days, I'm betting) so keeping them up late often backfires.

Weissbluth recommends putting the baby to sleep after two hours of being awake, and doing whatever it takes for the wild infant to zonk out (rocking, singing, glow-in-the-dark unicycle show). When the baby cries in opposition to this, let the crying go on for five to twenty minutes, and then try again. Kids from four to twelve months old should have two daily naps and be put to bed early. Weissbluth said you should not respond to the cries that follow at all, because "down is down." (That is the title, by the way, of the blues album my baby will be putting out later this year.)

The No-Cry Sleep Solution

The No-Cry Sleep Solution is a ten-step program to getting your baby to sleep. Its creator, Elizabeth Pantley, recommends developing a "sleep log" (a.k.a. the ramblings of a crazed insomniac), working with your baby's biological rhythms, and developing individual solutions that match your parenting style. As a bonus, this ten-step program gets your wild infant all ready for the various twelve-step programs he'll probably need as an adult.

Focal Feedings

This is a modified "cry it out" approach, which involves you waking the baby up at 11 P.M.—or whenever you're about to go to sleep—then feeding him and putting him back to sleep. If the baby wakes up before that time demanding food, have the non-milk-bearing partner try to settle the creature in the crib without picking him up. The idea is to get the baby used to longer periods of sleep, and also to teach him that he really can't just eat food all night and expect to be even halfway thin.

Scheduled Awakenings

This is a fascinating mind game you can play with your untamed baby, who, as we discussed, is operating at a mental disadvantage in the first place. In this method, you anticipate the times your wild infant wakes up, and set your alarm so you can beat him to the punch. This allows you to control the situation. Then start waking him up later and later, so he gets all mixed up and doesn't even remember to wake up and bother you!

Chapter 4

Soothing Your Wild Infant's Cries

One response that *Kingdomius infantius* specimens have to almost all situations in life is to just start bawling at the top of their lungs.

Why Your Wild Infant Cries

In his original habitat, your wild infant was not accustomed to foraging (or even whining) for food, or breathing air independently, or feeling his own foul, squishy waste contained in an ill-fitting sac Velcroed to his hindquarters. In prenatal times, known to your infant as "the good old days," all of this nasty business was efficiently handled by the body of the host organism, *Maternicus martyrius* (a.k.a. "Mommy").

Thus, your untamed baby may find it startling—even quite upsetting—to suddenly have to ask for these basic amenities. Thus, he reacts with anger, frustration, and extreme impatience. This phenomenon is known as inconsolability, or fussiness.

You must approach a fussy baby with care; this infant is quite enraged, and has no clue as to what he wants. An infant that does not know what he wants is very unpredictable, and may lash out in the following ways:

- 🐾 **Crazed thrashing of arms and legs**
- 🐾 **Projectile peeing (in *Babius boyus*) that seems uncannily aimed at your face**

- Blood-curdling, accusatory shrieks that tempt your neighbors to call the authorities

IF ONLY YOU COULD DO IT TOO

Can you, the adult human, imagine what your life would be like if you were to openly and extravagantly sob at every slight irritation? Here, for example, are a few vignettes from that life.

Your Boss: I'm going to need that report done today; the client has put a rush on the project. Would you be willing to stay late to get it done?
You: WWWWWAAAAAAAAAAH!!!! WAAAAAH!!!

Dry Cleaner: Mrs. Jones, I'm really sorry, but your dress won't be ready to pick up until next week.
You: WAAAAHHHHH! WAAAAA—(hiccup, hiccup)—AAAAAH!

You can imagine how well this would go over. But have some empathy for your wild infant—she doesn't yet have the tools to express herself in any other way. Crying is her primitive language, and therefore her only option for expressing herself.

(Well, she could just be quiet . . . that's an idea. Just saying.)

YOUR BABY-CRIES-TO-HUMAN DICTIONARY

One of the more frustrating aspects of caring for the wild infant in captivity is attempting to decipher her cryptic and primitive language. Although it seems clear that the little creatures have something rather important to say, the squalling cries emitted by *Kingdomius infantius* specimens seem to be pure nonsense. The best an untamed baby can produce is a mind-bending, existential wail that translates loosely to "I need something-or-other; I completely lack the knowledge and motor skills to help myself; and I deeply resent being born. Thanks a ton, a-holes."

However, many years of diligent studies by scientists, zoologists, and language specialists have allowed for some loose speculation as to the meaning of the various vocalizations made by the baby species:

- **Tired**—This is a sporadic, particularly deranged-sounding whimper, filled with dramatic hiccup-y sounds; eye rubbing; and guttural, low-pitched mutterings. This cry almost sounds as if the baby is trying to talk to herself, if only she were smart enough to understand herself. This is punctuated by furious, red-faced shrieks, then sudden, almost narcoleptic sleep. Occasional musical tones in this cry suggest that it is a type of weird self-lullaby mechanism. Too bad it doesn't help anyone else get to sleep.

- **Sharp Pain**—A keening shriek, followed by a long, silent pause and another piercing shriek. You will definitely hear this vocalization when your infant is vaccinated, or when a gas bubble is seeking escape from her stomach, or when you have the audacity to take her temperature using a rectal thermometer.

- **Hunger**—Short, repetitive, urgent cries, often accompanied by a creepy attempt to breastfeed from a man-boob or your mother-in-law's neck wattle.

- **Pooping**—A determined grunt, with vague undertones of pride (hey, the baby is actually accomplishing something for once!). This may coincide with what is known as the "gas smile." May happen while the untamed infant is eating. Note: Be sure to teach her that as an adult, she can't poop where she eats, metaphorically and otherwise.

- **Hot, Sick, Feverish**—This sounds, frankly, weak and whiny. You will find yourself thinking your wild infant is kind of a wuss until you realize she's not feeling well. Then you'll feel like a grade-A jerk. May go along with the "sharp pain" shriek if you use a rectal thermometer.

- Anger or Frustration—This is simply an all-encompassing scream of pure, blood-curdling rage at the sudden, uncomfortable predicament of existing in the world. Seriously, she was just fine hanging out in the womb. Can't you let her back there? It looks like there's still room.

- Boredom—Life can get awfully dull when you can't focus your eyes, sit up straight, or even chew gum if you felt like it. This cry sounds like a random rotation from gurgling to grumbling to wailing. The crying often stops when you pick up the bored baby. Unless you, too, are boring.

Note: These cries, and their respective meanings, are liable to switch up entirely at a moment's notice.

MAKING IT STOP

There is no guaranteed trick or "cure" to make a wild infant stop crying—that would be equivalent to looking for a "cure" to stop an adult human from talking. And no one wants to do that, do they? Especially if the adult human in question is your female partner and she has just borne you a child and she is very hormonal, and hasn't slept in months, and she just needs to vent and what are you good for if you can't even listen to her?

Right-o, then. Back to the untamed infant. You see, crying isn't just crying for an infant, the way it is for us. Crying is infant talk. It's their sole mode of communication. So once you know what she is saying, you can try to "answer" her with this arsenal of soothing methods. Many of these methods are based on an attempt to re-create the primal habitat of the womb. Here are some great "answers" to the wild infant question:

- Rock—Many untamed infants appreciate a gentle horizontal rocking motion while in a state of extreme fuss. You can rock your infant in your arms, or invest in a rocker or glider.

Scientists speculate that the gentle rocking motion is similar to the rhythms of the womb. Also, the motion may lead to a burp, which, for babies, is truly one of the finer things in life. Note: By the time your offspring reaches maturity, it is important to make sure he understands that rocking back and forth until he burps is not cool.

🐾 **Make Skin-on-Skin Contact**—Wild babies tend to prefer direct contact with the naked chest of a parent. This could be due to the primordial syncing of parent/child heartbeats in the womb. Or it could be the simple fact that he is mere inches away from the All-You-Can-Drink Milk Buffet. Dads, don't worry about not having a food supply; your wild infant is very easily fooled. They might be suckers, but they are also suckers.

🐾 **Noise/No Noise:** This is a perplexing contradiction among *Kingdomius infantius* specimens. While fussing, some prefer noise, such as a parent singing or a vacuum cleaner (or a vacuum cleaner to Hoover away the traumatic memory of a parent's singing), and some prefer total silence. Still other infants prefer noise that's all about the absence of noise (white noise). Honestly, these poor creatures are the hottest of messes, and your guess is as good as theirs. Trial and error is the best approach. And by "trial and error," I mean, "so much error, it will feel like a trial."

🐾 **Take a Hike**—No, I don't mean leave. I mean put your wild infant in a front pack or other baby carrier, and head outside for some fresh air. The change of scenery might be refreshing to her, and the movement might calm her down.

🐾 **Dance**—If the weather isn't nice enough for going outside, hold your untamed infant close (making sure to support her head) and dance around the room with her. You can dance to music, or just hum, or dance silently. Your wild infant might judge your dancing or eliminate you from the final round, but that's still better than crying, right?

❧ Hello, Binky!—Wild infants are also calmed by sucking, which reminds them of the time not so long ago when they were last hoovering up some breastmilk. A pacifier is a so-called "happy medium" between overfeeding and undersoothing. Also known as "binkies," pacifiers are slightly controversial, and are often a topic of what are known as "Mommy Wars." (Mommy Wars, which will be addressed briefly later, are basically silly, time-wasting blogged arguments about parenting that you don't really need to worry about.) To pacify or not to pacify? That is the question, and only you and your infant can answer it. The American Academy of Pediatrics approves the use of binkies for the infant's first year.

ANCIENT SECRETS OF THE SWADDLE

In their first few weeks of existence, many specimens of *Kingdomius infantius* feel calmer, and less infuriated about being suddenly unleashed into the world, when you wrap them up snugly. I mean, even Jesus Christ's mom took the precaution of wrapping him up in "swaddling clothes" so he wouldn't pitch a fit, and he was supposedly one of the nicest guys ever.

Why Swaddle?

Swaddling your baby will contain his or her flailing arms and legs, and the heat from a slightly dryer-warmed blanket will calm him down. Other members of *Kingdomius infantius* will hate this, and will quickly let you know. These babies tend to grow into adult humans who "don't like to be tied down," or "want their space," that sort of thing. Good luck with that.

How to Swaddle

If your baby does like to be swaddled, see the following images to learn how to do it.

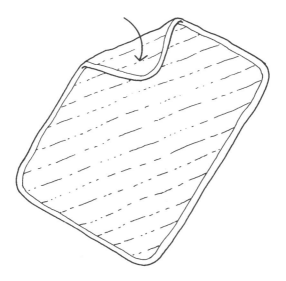

Position a square blanket like a diamond, and fold the top corner down.

Lay your baby on his back on the blanket, with the top corner just above his neck. Tuck one arm down and fold the blanket around his body and behind his back.

Fold up the bottom part of the blanket, folding down any excess that would be covering his face.

Tuck the other arm down and fold the remaining corner of the blanket around his body and behind his back.

Is He a Colic-aholic?

Sometimes, your wild infant will emit tortured cries for hours on end, piercing cries that seem to have no logical cause and don't respond to any soothing efforts. If this continues every day, at about the same time, it might be colic.

Doctors aren't exactly sure what causes colic, despite more than fifty years of research. It was once believed to be a type of abdominal pain (the word is derived from the Greek *kolon*, or colon, which refers to the large intestine). Newer theories have called this one into question, however.

Some researchers think colic could be a response to an intolerance of something in the adult human mother's diet, while others think it is related to an immature digestive system. Still other theories hold that it might just be a wild infant's way of trying to make sense of a busy day. Perhaps the worst-case scenario is that colic is just the normal amount of crying for some very stubborn, extremely emotional wild infants. Yikes.

Since no one really knows for sure what the hell colic is, a surefire solution to this problem is still quite a ways off. However, there are some soothing measures that seem to work for these infants. Sorry, that's the best modern science can do for you right now.

🐾 **Motion**—As is the case with other causes of crying, rocking, swinging in a baby swing, or riding in a stroller or car may be effective for colicky wild infants. Again, putting your infant on a train to someplace far away is the wrong kind of motion. *Wrong.*

🐾 **Medication**—There are some over-the-counter remedies that are said to provide relief from colic. Of course, there is no real evidence to support this, since this whole colic thing is as mysterious as a unicorn. Simethicone (brand names Mylanta or Mylicon) is one over-the-counter product that may help colic. It's given in the form of drops and breaks down gas bubbles. Hey, there's nothing wrong with breaking down gas bubbles, even if that turns out to have nothing to do with what colic is! Your doctor might also recommend other prescription drugs if the colic might be related to something like acid reflux.

🐾 Dietary Changes—If you are the maternal human parent and are nursing this colicky infant, try eliminating dairy products from your diet. If you are bottle-feeding, try switching to a soy-based formula (consult your pediatrician before doing this). An intolerance to cow's milk might be one of the things that causes infants to "be colicky."

🐾 Try standing on your head at all times while in the presence of your untamed infant. Colic may be caused by your infant's disdain for your normal right-side-up stance. Yeah, I made that one up. You considered it for a second, though, didn't you?

JUNGLE PLAYDATE

You know how you keep a spare tire in the trunk of your car in case you get a flat? Well, that's pretty much how the egret mom views her babies. She can only take care of two kids, but she has an "extra" just in case. Once she's confident that her first two are healthy and strong, she lets them go ahead and kill the third sibling. Hmm, can you imagine the sibling rivalry issues?

MOM: No, you can't kill your brother yet. Eat your worms, mister, and then we'll talk.

BABY EGRET #2: But you said *I* could kill him. How come Johnny gets to do everything first?

MOM: (Sighs) Look, whichever of you eats your worms first gets to kill your brother. How's that?

BABY EGRET #3: Um, Ma? What are you talking about?

MOM: Uh, don't you worry about it, Sparetireous.

Chapter 5

WILD BREASTCAPADES

If you are the female human in your tribe, you might already be clued in to the fact that you are a freestanding human milk factory, just waiting to be raided. You might have sensed this based on the fact that your boobs are gargantuan and you never had enhancement surgery. Perhaps the tightness and soreness of these huge boobs were what gave it away. Or maybe, it's the simple fact that milk is leaking out of your breasts on a fairly regular basis. As they say, the proof is in the pudding. But hopefully, you are not leaking pudding.

WHY BREASTMILK?

There are a lot of reasons why it's great—and just plain logical—to feed your baby your breastmilk. For one thing, this was milk meant specifically for her, and that's about as "natural" and "organic" as it gets. Second, the entire rest of the mammalian animal kingdom seems to get along just fine via breastmilk—you don't see *them* all lined up at Mrs. Cow's door, do you? Here are some other benefits of Grade A, human being person's milk:

🐾 **Paging Dr. Milk—Breastmilk provides antibodies that help prevent all sorts of illnesses in babies. Breastfed babies develop fewer allergies, and have a lower risk of diabetes. Seriously, the stuff is practically a pediatrician in a bottle. Except the bottle is your breast, and the idea of a pediatrician coming out of your breasts is a little bit disturbing.**

- Smarty Pants—Statistically speaking, wild infants that are breastfed are smarter and have enhanced cognitive development. However, a breastfed baby just told me this, so consider the source.

- Lipo-Suckling—Good news for adult human mothers: breastfeeding burns some serious calories—up to 500 in a session, according to *TodayHealth.today.com*. So as your infant takes in calories, you are producing and dispensing those calories. Otherwise, there's some super-slim cow out there getting your passive workout! OMG, she looks awesome!

- Breeders Digest—Breastmilk is easier for the wild infant to digest than formula. What this means is that your untamed infant's wild waste will be a little less . . . wild. Babies who drink breastmilk rarely have constipation or diarrhea, and their poop is less repulsive-smelling. It sort of resembles Dijon mustard in appearance and smell, and yes, it is taking all of my strength to avoid making some joke about, "Do you have any Grey Poop-on?" Wait, I guess I didn't avoid it.

- Free Is Cheap—For those who seek to save money while nourishing your young, the good news is that breastmilk is cheap. So cheap, in fact, that it is free. Also, you don't have to worry about transporting bottles or powdered mix to feed your baby when you go out. The food supply is right there—unless you forget your breasts. I hate it when I do that!

BREASTFEEDING HOW-TO

If you are the female human and your wild infant has just emerged from the womb, you might feel a bit awkward about immediately attaching his mouth to your nipple (how about getting to know each other a little first, huh?). If you're not ready to begin suckling your squirmy, unpredictable young right away, that's usually fine. Take a nap first if you like. Just make sure you dream about breastfeeding, so you'll know what to do when you wake up.

Conversely, the wild infant might be terribly disoriented from his arduous travels through your birth canal and out of your body, and might want a little bit of "space." Don't be upset if this happens—the little creature is probably overwhelmed from the hard work and annoyance of being suddenly evicted from his posh little home in your womb. Rest assured, he will get hungry eventually. And once he gets started, he probably won't stop for the foreseeable future!

Start by sitting up in bed, pulling up your hospital gown and settling a pillow on your lap. Make sure your back and elbows are supported. Females with large breasts can tuck a rolled-up washcloth or towel under the breast to prop it up if necessary.

The first time you suckle your wild infant, you will probably want to use the "football hold" or the "cradle hold." **Note**: The football hold does *not* entail throwing your infant like a football or attempting to punt him for a field goal.

Cradle hold

Football hold

- If it's warm enough in the room, try to initiate some skin-to-skin contact. Unwrap your infant and/or pull up his shirt so that his skin touches yours. Rotate the wild creature so that he faces your breast, making sure to support his head. With your other hand, form a *C* with your thumb and forefinger and cup beneath your breast. This *C* stands for "Come on and drink, already."

- Bring the wild infant close to your breast and lift up your nipple toward the baby. Tickle the baby's lips with the tip of your nipple. He probably won't laugh, but that's okay. It's not a particularly good joke.

- Wait until your wild baby opens his mouth really wide, and then shove your breast in as far as it will go. (Yikes! Things are going really fast all of a sudden, huh?) If you weren't quick enough with the whole "tickle and shove" maneuver, you might find that only the nipple is in the infant's mouth. That's not quite enough. If this has happened, it's no biggie. I probably didn't give you enough notice on the Big Shove. Just use your finger to break the suction and try again.

❀ Once your untamed creature is attached to the nipple, check his position. His mouth should cover a third of your areola, which is the darkened part of the nipple. Make sure your untamed baby's head is tipped slightly back, and his chin is pressed into your breast. The movements of the baby's chin and tongue are what pull out the milk. You should hear sucks and swallows until the hungry little mammal has drained the breast like a little milk vampire.

When he has drunk it all, you will stop hearing swallowing, and maybe instead he will be saying, "WTF? Got milk, biatch?" If your infant is a subtler type, he might just continue to work his mouth or jaw, to no avail. At this point, you will know it is time to switch breasts. Let him take a burp break in between breasts. Breast, burp, breast—what a life! If your infant is a guy, he will aspire to this lifestyle forever and ever!

KEEP IT COMING

In the first week of your wild infant's life, you (or the female of your tribe) are going to want to milk yourself like you are the only dairy cow at the Cold Stone Creamery. Frequent suckling stimulates production, and keeps you in the breastmilking biz.

Here are a few things to keep in mind as you begin your temporary career as a mother suckler. (Males of the tribe, you may skip this part and go find some other way to burn the hundreds of calories your partner will be burning from her boob muscles. May I suggest cleaning the house?)

- **Milk Is Fashionably Late**—It will take a few days for your "real" milk to show up. (Milk is notoriously late—what a jerk! Maybe if it didn't spend all its time making those ridiculous mustaches on people's faces, it would get places on time.) Actually, for the first few days, your untamed creature will be feeding on colostrum, which is a yellowish fluid that isn't nearly as gross as it sounds.

- **About That Yellow Stuff**—Colostrum is jam-packed with antibodies, and will give your feral infant protection against all sorts of viruses and nasty infections. It's also nature's laxative, and will basically flush out a pantload of black, tarlike waste that's been accumulating since before your creature's birth. Lovely. This stuff is called meconium, and it *is* as gross as it sounds. Sorry.

- **Happy Hormone**—The initial suckling of your wild offspring will stimulate the release of prolactin, which is a hormone that relaxes you and triggers milk production. So basically, it will make you incredibly relaxed and superproductive. You need to get some of this stuff for the office!

- **Super Suckler**—For the first few weeks, you will need to suckle your feral offspring at least ten to twelve times a day. This equals about once every two hours. Yep, it's a job. If you start to get annoyed, repeat the mantra "Burning more calories than an elliptical trainer" and you will feel much better.

- **Drink Up**—While this mysterious offspring of yours is drinking, you are actually supposed to be drinking, too. Unlike your baby, though, you should not be feeding from a woman's breast (males of the tribe, do not even try to suggest this) or from a frozen margarita, even if that would really hit the spot right about now. Have a drink of water, milk, or juice.

- **Wrist Position**—Keep your wrist straight; don't flex the wrist supporting the wild infant's head. This may tip the young mammal down into an awkward feeding position, and also it will hurt the hell out of your wrist. Some moms like to use a nursing pillow to help prop the baby up and save the wear-and-tear on their arms—more on those later in this chapter.

- **Ouch**—Remember to use your finger to break the mouth-nipple suction before removing your wild infant's jaw from the breast. Just ripping the kid off will be like pulling off a Band-Aid, times a thousand.

- **Slurp and Burp**—Don't forget to burp the wild infant while feeding. Most newborn humans don't fully get the concept of eating in the beginning, and mistakenly think its cool to eat a bunch of air, too. Although the calorie-free status of air makes this logic understandable, the baby will soon learn that being full of air is not nearly as super as being full of food. (Note: Some infants are smart enough to bypass this whole "eating air" phase, and therefore are not big burpers. Conversely, some adult humans never stop with the burping, not ever.)

- **Ask for Help**—If you're not sure whether you are doing an effective job as a suckler, ask for help. You can go to a maternity nurse, a pediatrician, or even something called a lactation consultant (yes, they have consultants for *everything* nowadays).

BREASTFEEDING AFTER A CAESARIAN

It is possible that rather than expelling your wild, bloody infant out of your body through waves of excruciating pain, you got to go off into a magical little dreamland and wake up with the whole thing done and over with. Good for you, but you probably woke up feeling like your head weighed 800 pounds and you'd been stabbed repeatedly in the midsection. In other words, you're going to be in pain, one way or the other. Pick your poison (actually, you probably won't get to pick).

Breastfeeding a newly spawned wild infant might be a tad more challenging when you're half-blotto from anesthesia and have a six-inch gash in the middle of your body. Still, though, don't you want to have a genius baby without diarrhea, constipation, or allergies? You know you do! Here are some tips on how to suckle after major invasive surgery.

- ❧ **Wake Up, Buttercup**—It is very possible that like you, your wild infant will be a bit out of it due to the anesthesia, which you passed along to her free of charge. You will probably need to keep waking the poor thing up so she stays alert while suckling. This could be problematic if you, too, keep falling asleep. Maybe the male human of your tribe can take turns pouring buckets of cold water on your heads, although in doing so, he may place his life at risk. Or, maybe you and the little mammal should just take some time and sleep it off. Either way, the anesthesia should be out of her system within a day or two.

- ❧ **Get Some Meds**—Female birth-givers, there is no need to be a heroine about pain relief. (There is also no need to take heroin for pain relief.) Your doctor will gladly give you pain medications within the first few days. Although small amounts of this will be passed along to your wild baby, it won't hurt her. Besides, it never hurts to take the edge off her "pain" of existing in the mortal universe.

- ❧ **Side Lying**—Positioning yourself for breastfeeding will also be a bit tougher after having had your internal organs messed with and all. Try the side-lying position: turn slowly on your side and put a rolled-up towel next to your incision (in case that crazy baby mammal of yours decides to kick!). Have your partner put the untamed infant on her side next to you, chest to chest, facing your breast. You'll need some help rolling over to offer the other breast, but that's what adult male humans are for. (Note: There is *no* need to dump buckets of water in this scenario, males.) Within a few days, you should be able to do the football hold. Go team!

🐾 Milk Delivery—Depending on why your infant was delivered by C-section, she might need to stay in the neonatal intensive care unit (NICU) for observation and treatment. If you'll be unable to breastfeed her right away, ask about getting a breast pump. This will allow you to get the milk factory going and crank out some of that healthy yellow liquid that contains all those nutrients. Make sure that this stuff gets delivered to your baby over there; you don't want the hospital staff guzzling it down like it's Red Bull.

WHAT TYPE OF FEEDER IS YOUR WILD INFANT?

As with animals who live in the wild, there are various categories of eating styles among infants. These are often based on the innate personality traits of the feral offspring in question, and may or may not be predictive of your young's future personality and style. Some animals are delicate, slow eaters; others are always in a rush. Some have four stomachs for digestion; others happily consume their momma's vomit. It takes all kinds.

The first five categories of human sucklers were named by scientists at Yale University, so if your infant happens to be one of those, you can feel extra fancy-schmancy. Your child can go around calling himself a "Yale gourmet" and no one will need to know he's talking about how he used to slurp from his mommy's boob. It sounds a little less sophisticated that way.

Barracuda

The fish that bears this name is known as a "voracious, opportunistic predator" that tears off chunks of flesh with its fanglike teeth. Barracuda fish aren't terribly intelligent, though, and are known to mistake shiny things for prey. Seriously, they eat diamond rings and stuff.

You are lucky that your "barracuda infant" does not yet possess fanglike teeth, but he's pretty voracious and opportunistic. These infants latch on and feed ravenously for ten to twenty minutes. This type might start to freak you out, but no matter what, don't offer him your engagement ring.

Excited Ineffective

This type totally spazzes out with excitement when he sees the breast, then proceeds to grab it, drop it in his frantic state, then throw a royal tantrum. You may have dated an "excited ineffective" before (I have). Hopefully for you, you did not marry one (no comment).

Procrastinator

This wild infant type looks at the yellowish colostrum and thinks, "Yeah, when that stops being the same color as snot and pee, I might start drinking it. Until then, let me take a rain check." Be patient with this infant—he is just holding out for the "real milk." Trying to persuade him that the icky yellow stuff is chock full of vitamins is very likely to be useless. Just keep pumping between feedings to keep the milk factory chugging along.

Gourmet

This baby will take a refined sip of milk, roll it around in his mouth, and comment on its "oaky yet smooth tannic notes combined with a fruity aftertaste." Basically, this kid is going to be a foodie or a wine connoisseur. He'll get his nutrition and all, but you'll probably have to listen to him blathering on about the inspirational texture of your milk first.

 **JUNGLE
PLAYDATE**

Tasmanian devils clearly aren't all that great at math. Despite the mom having only four nipples, these Australian marsupials give birth to up to thirty young at a time. Then the race is on to migrate to the mother's pouch, where these raisin-sized creatures compete fiercely to latch on to one of the four nipples. The lucky four stay attached to the nipples for the next five months (that's a lot of milk drinking!). As for the other twenty-six or so? Thanks for playing—better luck next time! The survivors emerge from the pouch with a full coat of fur and are left by their moms at the tender age of five months.

- -

The Rester

Look, eating isn't easy, at least not to a newborn wild infant who has never had to do anything, ever. For this individual, drinking milk is the equivalent of running a marathon while reciting all of the works of Shakespeare. It's just stressful. Therefore, the rester is going to need a lunch break from his lunch break. He'll eat, then sleep, then eat again. Get yourself something to read—it's going to be a long day for your boobs.

Billy Goat

This wild infant will head-butt, tug, or wallop you while drinking your life-giving milk. Gratitude is not this baby's strong suit. He may be annoyed that your milk flow is too fast or too slow. Everyone's a critic!

The Regurgitator

You'll think everything's going just dandy with this wild infant, until he pukes half of what he drank right back up onto you. Then he'll be ready to eat again. He's a lot like the Rester, except with the beginnings of quite the little eating disorder.

Barnacle

This baby gloms on to the food source and almost never lets go. This type may grow into a "needy" adult who insists on constant togetherness and matching clothes in a relationship. It might be difficult to detach from a barnacle type, literally and figuratively.

Sightseer

This wild infant has a wandering eye and a swiveling head, which continue to move around while attached to your nipple. This type of behavior usually begins in the fourth or fifth month and is either the beginnings of attention deficit disorder or potential monogamy issues. Try to teach this infant that if he wants to whip his head around suddenly, he can't take your poor nipple with him.

Desserter

This feral creature simply wants a bit of dessert after the main nursing course. He might drink for twenty minutes and then come back for a few more sips. Sadly, dessert will taste exactly the same as dinner.

GET THE GEAR!

Generally speaking, suckling the wild infant is about as basic and primal as can be: all that's needed is a hungry baby and two milk-filled breasts. All mammals have been doing this since the dawn of time. However, if you are the female human, you'll probably hear about all kinds of must-have, super trendy breast accessories from your friends and their mom blogs. So, go ahead, keep up with the Joneses. You'll have the most tricked-out mammaries on the block with this gear.

- A Nursing Pillow—These come either as a wedge that sits on your lap, a wide half-circle for your waist (great for football holds), or a "Brest Friend," which is a full circle to provide back support. Note: You can confide in your Brest Friend if you want, but personally, I would not trust that thing. I hear she's soooooo sick of supporting your back, and has been spreading some nasty rumors about you having hair on your nipples!

- A Nursing Stool—This is a low stool that lifts your legs just enough to relieve strain on your lower back. Maybe try this after you ditch that treacherous Brest Friend of yours.

- Flat Cloth Diapers—These can be used to absorb messy burps, drool, and any other emissions that fly out of the wild infant's maw.

- Electric Pump—Suckling your wild infant can get a modern overhaul when your boobs go electric, just like Bob Dylan did in the late 1960s. Your breasts will still be able to crank out their greatest hits the old way, but now you can pump out the classics at your convenience so your partner can take some of the late-night feedings, or you can actually leave the infant's side for more than an hour. Breast pumps range dramatically in features and cost, from simple one-side-at-a-time jobs to hospital-grade electric pumps. Decide how often you'll use it and compare features to know which one is right for you.

- Breast Pads/Shells—During the first few weeks especially, the female human is a rather leaky mammal. Not only is that messy, but it's wasteful. To absorb leaky milk, tuck some cotton or flannel breast pads into your bra. To collect that leaky milk, use silicone milk shells.

- ❧ Nursing Bras—These offer support for your cleavage, easy open-and-feed clasps, and remind your partner that your breasts are pretty much just milk machines for the time being.
- ❧ Casualwear—Oh, you'll want the most fashionable, easy-access, snap-front couture that's out this season. Or maybe one of those fun nursing dresses in the hottest new colors with discreet nipple slits. Those are sexy!

SORE NIPPLES

One drawback to suckling your wild infant is that your nipples might start to feel like they've been clamped by clothespins, nicked with razors, burned by a blowtorch, or some creative combination of the three. Usually, though, sore nipples are caused by improper positioning, or incorrect latch-on. In other words, it's your own damned fault.

The first thing you want to do is correct the positioning problem, or make sure your wild infant is being hooked up and disconnected from the nipple properly. After that, give these nipple-soothing solutions a whirl:

- ❧ Air-dry Your Nipples—You can use a breast shield, which will make your nipples feel like superheroes. Or, if you're into do-it-yourself projects, you can make your own charming breast shield out of two tea strainers (preferably plastic). Truly, no one will even notice that you've got a couple of tea strainers inside your bra. Madonna will wish she'd thought of this.
- ❧ *Jersey Shore* Your Nipples—Another approach is to let your nipples get a bit of sun. Find a private, sunny area, or use a sun lamp, and expose your nipples to some rays for three minutes several times a day. (Orange spray-tans do not work for this particular situation.)

- 🐾 **Put Breastmilk on Them**—What a nice little built-in solution! Breastmilk apparently has healing properties, so dab a little on the pain-wracked nipples. Your wild infant might be annoyed by the idea of you taking her food away. It's not like she smears filet mignon on her nipple, right?

- 🐾 **Tea Party**—Who would have known that the tea set Great Aunt Edna gave you for your wedding would get used so often on your boobs? Well, maybe Aunt Edna did—from personal experience! Ick. Anyway, try saving a cooled tea bag and putting it on your nipples for a few minutes. It's not only soothing, but classy.

- 🐾 **Lotion**—There are a lot of nipple ointments and lotions available. Choose one with lanolin, olive oil, or aloe vera gel. Avoid any lotions that contain pesticide residues. Your wild infant might be a bit of a pest, but you don't want to exterminate her!

- 🐾 **Ice Them**—Not only will ice dull the pain, but it will create those cold-weather nipples that the wild child can easily catch on to.

- 🐾 **Give It a Rest**—Try breastfeeding from only one breast to give the other nipple a little vacation time. You will still want to pump or hand-express the "resting breast." Some vacation!

SUCKLING ISSUES

You may run into some genuinely challenging issues while trying to suckle that voracious little beast you have produced. While some of these issues might seem more than a little gross and disturbing, they usually don't mean you should stop breastfeeding. Did you really think you'd get off the hook that easily?

Clogged Milk Duct

Clogged milk ducts are passageways that have gotten stopped up. You will feel a small lump in your breast, and it may be painful. Try putting a warm washcloth over the lump for five minutes, then massage the lump gently, pushing the milk toward the nipple. Do not try to pop it like a big milk zit!

After you have massaged the lumpy duct for a while, nurse the hungry wild infant, making sure she is facing the clogged duct, and keep massaging. The more you allow the baby to suckle, the faster the duct will become unclogged.

Breast Infection (Mastitis)

A breast infection is something you will need to call the doctor about. Some signs of this include flulike symptoms, a low fever, red streaks or patches on the breast skin, pain in the breast, or a hard lump in the breast. Your greedy little infant won't cut you a break, though—she'll still want her dinner on schedule. And believe it or not, you should continue to nurse with the infected breast.

Your doctor may prescribe antibiotics, and might also advise you to go to bed, drink lots of fluid, apply warm compresses on the infected side, and keep breastfeeding. Male partners, this would be a super time to really help out and bring your lady some juice or a nice cup of tea. But don't use the tea strainers she puts on her nipples—that would be disgusting.

Thrush

Yes, you and your wild infant may have the unique joy of sharing a nipple-to-mouth yeast infection. Aww. Your nipples may be cracked and may burn during nursing. Your wild infant may have white patches in her mouth, and possibly in the diaper area, along with a "not-so-fresh feeling." To prevent producing a loaf of bread between the two of you, you should make sure your nipples and everything that touches them are clean: use a nipple wash (1 teaspoon of vinegar mixed with 1 cup of water) or a prescription cream that stops yeast from reproducing.

PUMP START

Even if you, your partner, and your wild infant have gotten the suckling bit down to a science, there will probably be times where you'll want to have some spare product inventory stored up. For example, if it's the male human's turn to do a night feeding, or if the female human wishes to leave the house or take a few hours to do something other than be a milk sweatshop.

For this reason, the female of your tribe might want to crank out some milk for a rainy day. To do this, you will use a suction device that simulates the suckling of your wild infant, minus the biting, drooling, or vomiting.

Back in the olden days, there was no such thing as breast pumping, and to this day, other species of animal generally do not pump milk. But they don't need to go back to work, do they? Or if their job is to hunt buffalo or gazelles, it's always "take your kids to work day." Not to mention, they have, like, six nipples.

THE LETDOWN

What you need most for pumping is a "letdown," which, in wild infant world, does *not* mean a crushing disappointment. Letdown is a reflex that triggers the release of milk. Once this reflex kicks in, it can be set off by all sorts of crazy things, such as the sound of any baby crying. Even thinking about suckling might cause you to start oozing milk. It's beautiful and really creepy at the same time. You might like to look at a photo of your wild infant, or listen to music (luckily for you, about 75 percent of popular songs include the word "baby"). Hanging around your male adult partner as he behaves like a helpless, whiny infant may work, too. Just don't let him have any of the precious beverage.

Pumping Tips

Now that you know the historic and zoological context of pumping, as well as the mechanism that makes this phenomenon occur, you will want to prime the pump and start cranking it out ASAP. Here are some tips for beginning the fabulous adventure of pumping:

- 🐾 **Power Pump**—If you have difficulty with letdown, you might need a powerful, hospital-grade pump. You can rent these from a hospital, obviously, or from a lactation consultant. Women with breasts that let down at the drop of a hat can use a simple hand pump or no pump at all, since they are able to spurt milk just by looking at any bald guy who's not particularly tall. Portable "briefcase-style" pumps might be okay for the "executive pumper," but they aren't as strong as the less stylish models. Also, when considering stylishness, remind yourself that *it's a breast pump*. How stylish can it be?

- 🐾 **Pump Time**—It's generally best to begin pumping when your baby is at least a month old and is settled into a regular feeding schedule. You should pick a time that's in between the normal suckling time (for example, an hour after he's nursed, and an hour before you expect to suckle him again). Or maybe your wild creature has turned his nose up at a milk serving—in this case you can pump out a whole feeding.

- 🐾 **Keep It Clean**—Use clean pump equipment and bottles. Wash them with hot, soapy water and air-dry on a clean towel.

- 🐾 **Start Slow**—Start the pumping machine on the minimum setting, and then crank it up slowly until you're getting the milk. If you are using a single pump, pump on each side for five minutes. Or, if you are a multitasking female human, you can get an adapter that lets you milk both breasts simultaneously.

STORING THE PRODUCT

Once you have produced this spare liquid nutrition, you should store it in a safe place. Unfortunately, it doesn't come out of you conveniently stamped with an expiration or "suck by" date. Here are some guidelines for storing this lovely beverage you made.

- 🐾 Hot Stuff—Generally, breastmilk is good at room temperature for six to ten hours. This varies based on the temperature of the room. If it's hot enough to fry an egg, it's probably hot enough to froth your milk into a latte cappuccino. That'll only attract all those coffee shop hipsters to your house, and who needs that?
- 🐾 Cold Storage—You can keep breastmilk in a small fridge or cooler at work until you get home, but make sure the office food thief doesn't drink it behind your back. Is it unprofessional to label the stuff "Susie's Breastmilk— *Hands Off*"? Maybe so, but just think, if you get fired, you won't even have to pump at work! Overall, the Beverage of Champions can be kept unfrozen in a fridge for three to eight days.
- 🐾 Breastcapades on Ice—You can freeze breastmilk in a freezer with a separate door from the fridge for between one and four months, or in a freezer that is in the same compartment as the fridge for two weeks. If you put it in a chest freezer, it can be stored for six months. Breastscicles, everyone!

Thawing Frozen Milk

Thaw your wild infant's frozen milk by transferring it into the fridge for up to twenty-four hours. Once you're ready to serve it up, warm it by running it under warm water. Do not microwave your wild offspring's frozen milk. You should also remember to mix it back together by shaking or swirling it, or else the fat will rise to the top and your untamed young will get all cream. Not only will this make him overly full and deprive him of necessary fluids, it will totally ruin him for half-and-half cream later on.

SUPPLY AND DEMAND

Remember, if your breastmilk supply is running low, the best solution is to pump after each feeding with a strong electric pump. When it comes to milk production, it's all about supply and demand. So if you demand more from your breasts through pumping, they will be an awesome supplier!

The "Shake Vs. Swirl" issue seems to be the focus of an ongoing debate. Pro-Swirl advocates caution that shaking thawed breastmilk disturbs the structure of the unique protein chains that make breastmilk the awesome food that it is. These folks recommend "gently swirling" it instead. Although these "Swirlers" raise a valid point, they're also a teensy bit dramatic—shaking the milk doesn't make it go bad, it just diminishes its perfection. Besides, "gently swirling" puts you at serious risk of looking like a pretentious, wine-tasting weirdo over your own breastmilk (Note to self: potential sequel to *Sideways*? Start working on screenplay ASAP).

If you're not sure whether your "breastmilk remix" should involve shaking or swirling, a brisk swirl to recombine the cream and the milk is a good compromise.

Serving the Pumped Milk

You should serve the breastmilk to your wild infant in a bottle or cup, if he is old enough. Although your little feral creature might not be accustomed to a bottle at first, it will help that he is familiar with his favorite drink. The male and female human can work together on feeding a wild infant from a bottle. Be sure to introduce your wild infant to bottle-feeding at some point after the third week and before the eighth week. Timing is everything when it comes to starting a baby on a bottle.

Bottoms up, you crazy little creature!

Chapter 6

FORMULA FOR SUCCESS

Although breastmilk is the most natural feeding solution for wild infants, some female humans don't suckle their young in this way. The female might be taking a medicine that would pass into the breastmilk and harm the wild infant, or maybe she had significant breast surgery in which the milk ducts were cut (breast augmentation usually is not a problem). Moms who have highly contagious diseases also should not breastfeed.

Sometimes, a *Maternicus martyrius* just doesn't feel comfortable with the idea of breastfeeding, and that is okay! You should not allow yourself to be guilted or bullied by other people's notions of what you should do with your boobs. Just feed that crazy, ravenous creature before he eats you, okay?

FIND THE RIGHT BOTTLE

Once you've decided to feed your baby formula, your first step is to choose your bottle. Just like in those adorable videos you see of zookeepers feeding baby pandas, it's important to find the one that works best for your particular creature. Unlike the baby panda, though, your infant's bottle-feeding session probably won't be YouTube–worthy. I mean, come on—a baby panda is practically a miracle! Pandas only mate, like, once a year tops, and only after zookeepers throw them together and pipe Barry White into their enclosure round the clock. What's more, there's only a three-day window when they even *want* to do it. Can you say the same about you and your partner? Actually, don't answer that, okay?

Instead, let's just consider these bottle selection factors.

Bottle Materials

The three main types of bottles are glass, plain plastic, and plastic with disposable liners. However, makers of baby bottles have all sorts of crazy variations on this, and you can find short bottles; fat bottles; long, thin bottles; bottles with a bend in the middle; bottles with tubes inside; and bottles with handles. The main goal of all of these bottles is to make it harder for the baby to gulp air. There are advantages and disadvantages to each, so you should choose whatever seems to work best for you and your untamed infant.

Safety First

To be on the safe side, avoid feeding your wild infant from a bottle that was manufactured using Bisphenol A (BPA), a chemical used to create the plastic polycarbonate. BPA is a synthetic estrogen, and was formerly used by most baby bottle manufacturers. There have been debates on whether BPA can increase risk of cancer, diabetes, and obesity. Because of the hormonal component, some people think BPA can also lead to early puberty. And we all know that the only thing more difficult than a wild infant is a wild adolescent! You can find plenty of BPA-free bottles in today's market. For an update on these products, visit *www.safemama.com.*

Pick Your Nipple

When selecting a nipple for your bottle, you should first consider what your infant knows already. If your wild infant will be suckling from a bottle from Day One, you can choose the "standard" nipple like those that you may have suckled from yourself, once upon a time. But if you are switching from breastfeeding to bottle-feeding, you should choose a nipple that is similar in appearance to those of the *Maternicus martyrius*.

You might want to allow the wild infant to "test drive" a few different nipple shapes to see which she prefers before you buy an armload of one kind. If you can't find a good variety at your local store, go online and Google some nipples (there's a phrase our moms probably never used). Male humans: You might want to do this with your female partner present, so that your "nipple search" does not lead to a misunderstanding when she finds it later.

Color and Material

You'll also discover different colored nipples—brown or clear—and different materials—silicone or rubber. If you can find a silicone nipple in your desired shape, choose the silicone. Rubber has a distinct taste that the wild infant might dislike. Also, it is harder to tell if the rubber nipples are clean, since they're brown and all.

Holey-Moley

Another nipple difference is in the hole. Some nipples have many holes, while others have just one. Some holes are small, while others are gaping. Smaller, "slow-flow" holes are meant for newborns, while larger holes are meant for more advanced slurpers. More important than age is how much your wild infant is used to guzzling at one time. If you want to check on the flow a certain nipple provides, turn the bottle upside down and shake it a couple of times. There should be one spritz followed by slow, steady drops. To adjust the flow, you can loosen or tighten the bottle's ring. Observe the flow your feral creature enjoys, and make adjustments accordingly.

MORE BOTTLE-FEEDING GADGETS

Surely you didn't think that bottles and nipples would be all the gadgetry you'd need, did you? Don't be silly! You need a bunch of other supplies so that you can prepare, clean, and travel with your wild infant's bottles. However, you probably won't need everything on this list, unless you are some sort of bottle-feeding overachiever. Or unless your wild infant is so frighteningly ravenous, you just want to carry extra random stuff to throw into her gaping jaws!

- ❁ **Adequate Bottle Supply**—This would seem to fall into the "duh" category, but having a wild infant around pretty much devalues the meaning of the word "duh," since you'll be saying it approximately every other heartbeat. So, regarding bottles: you will need eight 4-ounce bottles for a newborn, and eight 8-ounce bottles for an older untamed baby. For an adult, you'll need a 40-ounce bottle of malt liquor.

- ❁ **Bottle Brush**—These special tools are for cleaning out your baby's bottles, and usually go with specific brands and shapes of bottle. After you're done cleaning the bottle with the brush, you will need to clean the brush, too, or else what's the point?

- ❁ **Graduated Pitcher**—Use this to mix up some batches of formula. Because nothing says "refreshment" on a hot summer day like a tepid pitcher of formula!

- ❁ **Dishwasher Basket**—You will use this for holding rings and nipples in the dishwasher. Later, you use it to wash sippy cups, baby utensils, and any other tiny wild infant–related feeding accessories. One disadvantage: if you are trying to wean your savage off a pacifier, you no longer have a perfect excuse to "lose" the binky in the dishwasher.

- ❁ **Bottle Warmers**—These pads heat up when pinched. Just like your wild infant does. Pinch the infant at your own risk.

❖ **Travel Formula Dispenser**—You will need some sort of dispensing unit for doling out the right amount of formula on the road. You might use a plastic case with multiple compartments for premeasured powdered formula, or a two-chambered bottle, one for powdered formula, one for water. Another option is to premeasure formula into bottle liners, twist-tie shut, and mix with premeasured water kept in a separate bottle. A final option is to try not to go on any extended trips with the wild infant until she can eat like a grownup human and you don't have to do all that godforsaken mixing and measuring. Just throwing it out there.

WHAT'S FOR DINNER?

Once you've got all of your bottle-and-nipple hardware, as well as your elaborate chemistry set for mixing and traveling with formula, the next step is to choose the beverage itself.

The Original Formula

If you happen to be using bottles to serve up prepumped breastmilk, your dilemma is solved. Just trick your wild infant into thinking the bottle is a breast, and let him guzzle away. It'll taste the same; he'll just wonder why your boobs are now long, made of plastic, and marked with ounce measurements. As an adult, he may be attracted to women with ounce-measured bottle breasts. But that will be a beautiful thing, because women with bottle breasts often have a hard time finding a mate (not to mention a decent-fitting bra).

Pumping Iron

If you don't have breastmilk available, you will need to choose a formula for your toothless little creature. No matter which kind you choose, it should be fortified with iron.

Soy Versus Milk?

Currently, there are milk-based and soy-based formulas available for suckling your wild infant. However, recent research has found that soy-based formulas don't lower the risk of allergies or colic, as previously thought. The American Association of Pediatrics says that soy-based formulas should only be chosen in the following three situations:

1. **Veganism**—You and your human partner are strict vegans (you do not eat red meat, poultry, fish, or any products that come from animals, such as eggs or dairy). If you plan to teach this wildly voracious creature your plant-loving ways, soy formula is an option for you. Either that, or letting your wild infant eat your arm off. But wait, that's meat, right?

2. **Lactose Intolerance**—Your feral offspring has been diagnosed with lactose intolerance, which is more common in older children and adults (it's considered rare in infants). Babies with lactose intolerance are not just allergic to cow's milk; they can't digest the sugar lactose found in cow's milk and cow's milk–based formula. And they don't just sneeze when they drink the stuff—they have epic, grosstastic diarrhea. Soy-based formulas are lactose-free.

3. **Galactosemia**—Your untamed creature has congenital galactosemia, which is also a rare condition. This disease means the baby doesn't have the enzyme that converts galactose, one of two sugars found in lactose, into glucose, a useful sugar to the human body. For these wild ones, drinking breastmilk, cow's milk, or any other milk products can cause serious damage. A buildup of galactose can cause eventual blindness,

severe mental impairment, growth deficiency, and death. These wild infants must absolutely consume soy-based formulas and steer clear of the galactose!

Hypoallergenic Formulas

Another possibility for some wild infants who cannot tolerate cow's milk formulas is a hypoallergenic formula, which is not the same as a soy formula. These are usually amino acid–based or hydrolyzed. These formulas can cost up to three times more than the typical cow's milk or soy-based formulas. However, if they work and your crazed infant seems to like them, you might want to pony up for the expensive liquid. Just remember it, so that someday, when your adult kid offers to buy you a drink, you pick the most expensive cocktail on the bar menu.

PLAYDATE

If there's one animal in the world that deserves a "#1 Dad" coffee mug, it's the Emperor Penguin. Not only does this guy dress up in formalwear for every occasion, he also performs an amazing act of dedication and sacrifice for his kids. Once the mom penguin lays the eggs, she is, understandably, pretty hungry. So she and the other females leave the eggs with the dads and travel across the ice to replenish themselves in the ocean. It's like a giant girls' spa getaway. Meanwhile, the dads balance the eggs of their precious young on their feet, and huddle together for three months in subzero winds. They don't eat and they barely move. Mom gets back just in time for the babies to be born, and only then do these dads get their long-awaited lunch hour!

- -

How to Mix and Prepare Bottles of Formula

Once you've narrowed down the bottle, the nipple type, and the actual drink being served, the next step is to mix it up like you're Tom Cruise in *Cocktail*. Although I'm pretty sure no trendy mixologist's bartending bible begins, as does this list of instructions, with the phrase "boil the nipples."

Step #1: Boil the Nipples

Before the first use, you'll need to boil the nipples and other bottle parts. (This not only sterilizes them, but eliminates that plastic flavor. I offer my advance apologies to your wild infant if she loves the taste of plastic.) There is probably no need to sterilize them again after that, as long as your wild infant is healthy and you have a chlorinated water supply.

Water from a well might be an issue—you should probably have your well water tested for safety, or boil the bottles in a pot for five minutes before each use. And wow, if you are pumping well water to formula-feed your wild infant, you really must like doing things the old-fashioned way! Maybe you should just hitch up your horse and buggy and go buy some Evian!

Anyway, after the first use, you can just run the bottles through the dishwasher or hand-wash them in soapy water.

Step #2: Mix It Up

Wash your hands, wipe the top of the formula can, and mix the formula exactly as the instructions say to (unless it's ready-made formula). Too little water can cause dehydration, but too much means your wild infant might not get enough calories. If you are concerned about the content of your tap water, use bottled water. Don't use sparkling water! Babies have enough trouble with air bubbles as it is.

Step #3: Pour Formula Into Bottle

If you've seen bottle-feeding on television, you might think you have to warm the bottle for this wild infant. Nope. Think of all the other wild beasts in the animal kingdom. Do they heat up their milk before they serve it? I think not! I mean, granted, I've seen a mama bear approaching my microwave with some porridge before, but she always ends up making it "too hot." Silly bear!

The fact is, most wild infants come to prefer whatever temperature bottle they get most often. Certainly, if a baby is willing to drink from a cold or room temperature bottle, the whole process will be faster and easier. Give it a try before you default to warm milk.

Perhaps you have a picky little bugger, or one who has simply seen too many old movies. If you have a warm bottle holdout for whatever reason, go ahead and heat the milk. Then do the old-fashioned "wrist test" where you shake a few drops on your wrist to test the temperature. If the formula feels hot, it's too hot. If you put the stuff in the microwave, shake the bottle well so there are no "hot spots." Also, avoid putting glass bottles, which can crack, in the microwave. Plain plastic (without liners) bottles are best.

BABY BOTTLE BLOOPERS

Every parent of a wild infantile creature will make mistakes, and most will make plenty (just ask your kid's future therapist when he's forty!). But when it comes to bottle-feeding, or, as I call it, "hitting the bottle," there are several easily avoidable mistakes. One of them is referring to it as "hitting the bottle."

Here are some others:

- ❧ Repeat Boilings—There's no need to boil bottles to sterilize them each time. This is pretty much a waste of time and hot water. Just like the movie *Hot Tub Time Machine*.

- ❧ Changing the Water-to-Formula Ratio—Look, there are instructions available for a reason. Follow them. Just because you're doing all this mixing and pouring and measuring doesn't make you Marie Curie. Messing around with the water-to-formula ratio can cause you to dehydrate or starve your wild infant. Or just really piss him off.

- ❧ Boiling Water for Powdered Formula—There's no need to boil water from your tap unless it is known to have problems. In which case, why not go the next step and use bottled water? If your tap water is A-okay, there's no need to boil and toil.

- ❧ Microwaving the Bottle with the Top Still On—Can you say, "Pop Goes the Nipple?"

- ❧ Microwaving Breastmilk—This kills the valuable antibodies it provides. Nice job, antibody murderer.

- ❧ Forgetting to Shake the Bottle—Don't forget to shake a microwaved bottle to get rid of hot spots. Just think of the song, "Shake Your Booty," but replace it with "Shake Your Bottle." Your dignity and coolness might die on the spot, but your wild infant will have a nice, safe bottle of formula.

- ❧ Giving Out Bottles to Go—Never give a wild infant a bottle to hold in the crib. This can lead to tooth decay or ear infections, especially when the baby falls asleep with the thing still in his mouth.

- ❧ Overtightening the Nipple Ring—Do not screw down the nipple ring too tightly. This obstructs the flow of milk and seriously annoys your wild infant. (Note: If you have a "nipple ring" from your crazy days of body piercing, this is *not* the kind of nipple ring I am referring to. You do not need to screw that in, or not screw it in, or mess with it in any way, especially if you're bottle-feeding. Carry on!)

🐾 Bottle Propping—Don't prop up a bottle to feed the wild infant. If the wild creature is too young to hold a bottle, someone should be holding the bottle for him. Propping up bottles for a visually impaired, motor skills–free infant (a) can cause choking, and (b) is just plain lazy. Hold the bottle, will you?

🐾 Pressuring Your Infant—Don't peer pressure the wild infant to finish a bottle. Breastfed babies pretty much suckle until they are full, so there is no reason it should be any different for bottle-fed infants. Especially do not chant "Chug! Chug! Chug!" as you pump your fist at the infant. There is no need to haze your baby. He's in, whether you like it or not.

BOTTOMS UP!: HOW TO BOTTLE-FEED

Whether you nourish your baby from a bottle or from a pair of huge bazonkers, feeding your wild infant is a great chance to bond with this odd little creature. Bottle-feeding, however, can be especially great as a bonding experience between the wild infant and the paternal figure (*Paternicus cluelessicus*).

Dudes, I realize that I presented the breastfeeding instructions from a distinctly female vantage point. For that I apologize. I promise that when men grow breasts that squirt milk out of them, I will rewrite that section immediately. But for now, in the interest of fairness, I will present the bottle-feeding protocol from the perspective of the male human parent. Enjoy.

🐾 Sit Down—Settle into a comfortable chair with a table nearby. This is so you can rest the bottle there when you stop to reposition the wild infant. Turn off the phone and try to minimize other distractions, even checking the score of the game and playing online golf.

* **Position Yourself**—Hold your wild infant close to your beer belly, positioning his head in line with the rest of his body. He should be at about a 45-degree angle, so that his ears are higher than his mouth and his head tips back slightly. If your baby spits up during the feeding, adjust the angle a bit, but don't lie him all the way flat. If you spit up during the feeding, swallow it, dude! You're supposed to be a man.

* **Do Several Girly Things**—Pick up the bottle, and then, with one finger on the hand holding the bottle, stroke the baby's cheek. (Do not let anyone take a picture of you caressing a baby's cheek; they will totally blackmail you.) When he turns toward you, brush his lips with the nipple (again with the blackmail advice).

* **Hook Up Your Infant**—Let your wild infant latch onto the nipple himself; don't stuff it in. (I realize that "stuff it in" might have been your personal motto for many, many years, but you are going to have to switch it up now.)

* **Check His Form**—Make sure your wild infant is latched on properly to the bottle. The tip of the nipple should be in the back of his mouth. Hold the bottle securely so that it resists suction; otherwise, he won't get any milk out. He will find that really annoying.

* **Make Adjustments**—As he drinks, continually adjust the angle of the bottle so that the nipple is always filled with milk, not air. Don't tip the bottle up any more than you need to, since this speeds up the flow. Gulping babies tend to swallow air.

🐾 Burp Break—When your wild infant starts to fuss and squirm and pull away from the bottle, stop for a burp, and then let him try to drink again. You yourself might also want to stop for a burp. Don't get too weird about making sure he eats enough. He's going to eat as much as he wants, and when he's done, he's done, just like with breastmilk. Just because you can't get enough of nipples doesn't mean this little guy doesn't have a limit!

Chapter 7

BABYIUS MESSIUSSMELLIUS

In the beginning of his life, the wild infant will basically do four things: eat, sleep, pee, and poop. These are the four main tasks that you, as the adult human, must assist him with. Because even though he does these four things on a daily basis, he doesn't do any of them without your help. It's like he has four jobs, and he's not very good at any of them.

Technically, wild infants can certainly pee and poop on their own, but they need your help in cleaning, changing, and monitoring these functions. If you are a squeamish type, you might find this a bit, shall we say, challenging.

UR-INE BUSINESS

When you first begin breastfeeding your wild infant, one important way to figure out whether he's getting enough milk is to count how many wet diapers he has created in a twenty-four-hour period. So even if you're not really able to measure milk consumption on the intake end of things, you'll be sort of keeping track on the diaper end. Here are a few guidelines:

🐾 **Six to eight wet diapers in a twenty-four-hour period is good. That means your infant is definitely getting his fill and peeing it right on out. Congrats!**

THERE'S AN APP (FOR THAT CRAP)

Back in the olden days, you had to pull down infant pants, unpin the cloth diaper, and use your eyes, hands, and/or nose to determine the diaper's status. And really, who has time for *that* nonsense? Luckily, there are now disposable diapers available with a "wetness indicator" conveniently located on the outside. Yay! We never really needed five whole senses, anyway!

It seems that smartphone apps have also gotten in on the diaper-tracking action. There are several apps that calculate your diaper needs based on your baby's food intake. It's a very simple "what goes in, must come out" formula, and can help prevent highly unpleasant diaper shortages.

* There are variations on the number of wet diapers your infant might achieve. Some urinate every one to three hours, while others might pee only four to six times a day. If your wild infant is sick, or it's very hot out, he might urinate less and that is still in the normal range.

* Urination should not hurt (these are good words to live by in general, actually). If it seems your wild baby is freaking out like a cornered mountain lion while trying to pee, call the pediatrician. This could be a urinary tract infection. Most of you ladies will know what that's like (no fun!).

* If you see blood in your wild infant's urine or bowel movements, call the pediatrician to be sure it's nothing serious. In fact, in the first few days of life, a few spots of blood are normal. They can be from urates, which are normal crystals in a baby's urine that turn to a salmon color on the diaper. Talk to the doctor if you see blood spots after the first few days. In girl wild infants, the spots might also include a small amount of bloody vaginal

discharge caused by the hormones of the adult human mom. Again, this blood usually goes away within the first few days.

Poop Culture

Ah, pooping—for the newly birthed wild infant, this particular activity is front-page news. Sure, sleeping, eating, and peeing are super big deals too, but they don't quite compare to poop. For most humans, poop is the first thing we will ever create in life, and, sadly, for some of us, quite possibly also the last thing we create. For babies, poop is pretty much their crowning achievement until they are able to scribble with crayons.

Maybe it's for this precise reason that wild infants are so incredibly creative about the stuff. During your time as a diaper changer, you'll see this stuff in a wide variety of colors, textures, and shapes. Your baby is making it for you—look, Mom!—so rather than feeling like a lowly butt-wiper, you should feel like an inspiration. You are his Poop Muse.

Frequency

You can probably expect your untamed infant to soil several diapers a day, but there's a wide range of poop production that is considered normal. For example, your infant might have as many as ten bowel movements per day, or as few as one a week (what an efficient consolidator baby!). The general rule is that if the infant is eating well, seems comfortable, and is growing, you don't need to worry about the frequency of his poop.

Sights and Sounds

Do not be alarmed by sudden, explosive sounds produced by your tiny wild creature. He may be tiny and vulnerable-looking, but his bowels are capable of suddenly erupting with a loud gush of poop lava and sulfuric flatulence at a moment's notice. The loudness of the rumbling, the gaseous hiss, and the explosion is quite jarring to the new adult human parent. When you hear these natural disaster sounds emanating from your infant's flanks, it is time to get to the changing table and face the mustardy music.

What You'll Encounter on Your Diaper Safari

Here are the two main types of fascinating creations your wild infant will make for you.

Tarred and Feathered

As previously mentioned, the first poop of all wild humans resembles tar—it's black (or dark green), super-sticky, and hard to clean. This stuff, called meconium, accumulates in the intestines of the wild infant during his carefree days in the womb, and must exit his body once he exits your body. Until this tarry paste gets out of the wild infant, he won't be able to digest food properly. With luck, for your sake, this meconium purge will take place at the hospital under someone else's hygienic watch. If not, you will be wiping it off at home.

Meconium is not as easy to wipe off as standard feces. It's stubborn. You might find yourself emptying an entire pack of baby wipes or using gallons of plain water, and that *still* might not be sufficient. Try some baby oil on a cotton ball. Once you've managed to get this tarry stuff off, dispose of it normally. Do not try to repave your street with it.

Pass the Mustard

After the tarry black stage, your wild infant will switch up the color palette and begin to produce feces in a yellowish-green hue. If you are breastfeeding, it will resemble seeded, runny Dijon mustard. If you are feeding your feral creature formula, what he will give you in return will be more tan in color, and thicker than peanut butter. It will not yet be "chunky style" at this particular stage.

The Basics You Will Need

It wouldn't be a wild infant bodily function if it didn't necessitate you buying a bunch of must-have accessories. Here is what you will need:

- 🐾 A changing table that is tall enough so you don't strain your back while changing the diaper. That's just nice for you, the wild human parent.
- 🐾 A diaper pail for whichever kind of diaper you prefer.
- 🐾 A wide variety of changing pads with buckles or straps— one for the changing table; one for travel; and a large, waterproof pad for "naked time." (Note: Be sure your wild infant knows that as an adult, he should not feel comfortable keeping a waterproof pad for his "naked time.")
- 🐾 Two pad covers in rotation (one on the changing pad, one in the wash). These will obviously get dirty regularly.
- 🐾 Cream or ointment for diaper rash.
- 🐾 A sense of humor. If you don't have one of these, it can be acquired by spending a year or more changing wild infant diapers.

Support Our Poops!

As the brand-new adult human parent of a wild infant, you might not be aware of a phenomenon known as the "Diaper Battles." Yes, that's right—Diaper Battles. You see, as the human species has evolved, female specimens have taken to challenging one another over dominance and pecking order in the realm of parenting. These are called "Mommy Wars." They are carried out not on the plains of the Serengeti, but in a new virtual battleground known as "Mom Blogs." In these Mommy Wars, females often fight to the virtual death, with the defeated mom cruelly cast out of the community, her blog deleted, her followers gone. The other moms of the community then roll over in submission and obey the victor.

The battles within this war often involve the power of one female's parenting philosophy versus the other female's. They involve, for example, breastfeeding vs. formula feeding, TV vs. no TV, and disposable diapers vs. reusable.

Diaper Battles are a subset of the Mommy Wars waged by human females. Here we present the different camps in this particularly filthy war.

The Cloth Loyalists

Cloth diapers were once the only option for absorbing and catching your wild infant's waste. Then, technology and innovation moved forward and produced disposables. But later, it was discovered that disposable diapers are bad for the environment, and so cloth diapering made a comeback.

In addition to being more environmentally sound, cloth diapers can be cheaper, and some can be used for a variety of other purposes. Since they've become more popular, they're available in easier-to-use styles with snaps and Velcro, and you can find them in a wide array of colors, patterns, and sizes. Some experts think wild infants raised on cloth diapers tend to be potty trained sooner, since they can feel the wetness of their pee soaking the diaper. (Disposables wick the moisture away so the baby doesn't have to experience a sopping diaper.)

On the other hand, most daycare centers require disposable diapers, and many babysitters greatly appreciate them. So if you decide to kick it old-school, you should probably be the one cleaning the old-school poop. (In other words, don't saddle your babysitter with soggy cloth diapers and endless loads of laundry. She can't be making enough money for that.) In addition, some of the newer cloth diapering options are actually pretty pricey.

The Disposable Rebels

According to those in the Disposable Rebels camp, disposable diapers are easier to deal with, more intuitive to use, and less bulky under your wild infant's clothing. They also don't require accessories like liners and covers, and you won't need to make as much of an up-front financial commitment. Another attractive advantage of disposables is less laundry to do and fewer diaper changes. Those in the disposable camp also argue that cloth diapers require the use of a great deal of water and energy for washing.

However, most disposables are not biodegradable, and even eco-friendly disposables can't fully break down in an airtight landfill. Ew! "Airtight diaper landfill" definitely does not sound like a good perfume name!

Different Types of Cloth Diapers

If you decide to join the Cloth Loyalists, you have a few options about the type of cloth diaper you wish to use. There are different styles available, and they are fastened usually by Velcro or something called a Snappi (no, this is not a new, particularly ill-tempered *Jersey Shore* cast member—it's a cloth diaper fastener that works kind of like an ACE bandage fastener). Some types of cloth diapers come with their own fasteners for your convenience, so you can tell Snappi to kiss your BumGenius All-in-One.

Here are your choices in style for cloth diapers. They are all uber-fashionable this season.

🐾 Prefold Diapers

According to *www.thestorkwearhouse.com*, prefold diapers are the most economical type of cloth diaper. They're also considered the most durable, and can last through eight children. Also, if you raise eight children on cloth diapers, prefold diapers might come in handy later for polishing your sainthood medal. (I'm just assuming they hand out medals for sainthood. A gold watch, at least, would be nice.) Prefold diapers have a thick center and thinner edge sections, and are rectangular in shape. They can double as burp cloths and be used as inserts for pocket diapers. Prefold diapers require some sort of waterproof cover so that your wild infant's liquid waste doesn't soak right through to his adorable miniature jeans.

✿ Pocket Diapers

Considered a major innovation in cloth diapering, pocket diapers are what all the clued-in kangaroo moms would be diapering with if only they'd thought of it (and if they used diapers at all). Instead, baby wallabies let the feces fly right in Mama's pouch. That's real nice, kids! It won't be too embarrassing next time your mom goes digging in her pocket for loose change!

Pocket diapers consist of an outer layer of waterproof material and a comfy inner layer of microfleece or suedecloth. This keeps your infant dry and prevents diaper rash. In between those layers of your "hot pocket," you can "stuff whatever material you wish" to customize absorbency, StorkWearhouse.com reports. **Note**: Queso chicken and pepperoni are not recommended materials.

✿ Fitted Diapers

Fitted diapers are considered a "happy medium" between prefolds and pocket diapers. According to StorkWearhouse .com, these feature elastic and built-in fasteners, and are very comfortable for the wild infant. Best of all, they provide excellent protection against leaks and explosive events. Like prefolds, they require some sort of waterproof cover.

✿ All-in-Ones

All-in-one diapers are considered the easiest to use in the cloth diaper category, but according to StorkWearhouse.com, they tend to have issues with washing completely and drying efficiently. And really, how "easy" is a diaper that doesn't come totally clean? The whole idea of these things is to deal with yucko human waste in a relatively clean manner until that miracle called potty training occurs. So make it easy on yourself and find an all-in-one that washes well.

JUNGLE PLAYDATE

Although other species of animals might not have diapers, Mom Blogs, or Diaper Battles, they still take care of their baby's icky poop—often in extremely unsavory ways. According to Kol Medina of the *Bainbridge Island Review*, mother squirrels, left with no other way of handling her babies' number 2, clean it up by eating it. In addition, Mama Squirrel is kind (or masochistic) enough to lick the babies' butts in order to stimulate bowel movements. Actually, many species of animal do this for their infants. So moms, maybe it's just about time to stop whining about whatever type of diaper you decide to use. Just think of your sisters in the animal world. They're probably not even thinking about whether you're polluting their environment. They're thinking, "Damn, it's time to lick the baby's butt again."

- -

DISPOSABLE DOS AND DON'TS

Perhaps you're not ready to tackle the extra laundry that cloth diapering brings, or handle a Snappi, or stuff a "pocket diaper" with, I don't know, falafel, maybe. Whatever your reason, if you've decided to use disposable diapers, here are some tricks of the trade that will make this approach easier and more effective for you and your explosive little waste machine:

- If your wild infant still has her umbilical cord, fold the top of the diaper down to turn it into a "bikini" before fastening. Umbilical cord bikinis are hot!
- Buy a bunch of diapers in your wild infant's current size, and one bag in the next size up (babies grow fast!).
- Be sure the leg edges of the diaper are turned out, not folded back under the elastic of the diaper. This ensures a better seal. Sealed diapers are good diapers.
- If you are using disposables that fasten with adhesive tape, be sure not to get anything on the sticky part, such as lotions, water, powder, or poop. Any of these substances take away from the adhesiveness of the tape. If you're using ones with Velcro tabs, don't pull too hard or you might rip them off.
- When changing the diaper of a male wild infant, make sure his penis is pointed down toward the middle of the diaper. If you diaper his penis up, or tucked in one of the leg edges, there is no telling where the pee stream will wind up. Hint: It'll probably be on you.
- Current disposable diapers are pretty tough; they tend not to leak until they weigh more than your baby. And if you are carrying around a baby whose weight is more than half poop, your house must be starting to smell strange and your arms must be seriously buff. But seriously, you should change a diaper way before that, like when the diaper starts to get a little squishy. Not

changing diapers enough not only causes discomfort for your wild infant; it also causes little pellets of superabsorbent gel to burst out of the diaper, which are *very* difficult to get off your infant's skin unless you give her a full bath.

DIAPERING: STEP-BY-STEP

Once you've chosen the diapering material and style that works best for your wild infant, you will need to actually do this thing. Don't be freaked out; you can do this. It has been done by every human parent from your mother to your grandmother to Moses's mom, and all of those babies went on to become independent adults with normal bathroom skills. (I can't vouch directly for Moses, but there's no mention of him having number 2 issues in the Bible, so . . .)

Anyway, the time has come: you have your supplies and wild infant on the changing table, and regardless of where you stand on the Diaper Battles, the real war is between you and that poop. So face the enemy and vanquish it!

1. The first thing you must do is avoid looking disgusted or horrified at what your wild infant has produced. If you gag, turn the gag into a giggle; if you catch yourself grimacing, turn the grimace into a grin. You see, diaper changing is supposed to be fun for the wild infant; you want to convince him of this no matter how nauseous you might feel. Sing, turn on a baby mobile, or hold a toy in your mouth (but not if you're already feeling gaggy). Have your partner do a puppet show for the wild creature. Do whatever it takes to keep the little wild one happy and lying relatively still on his back.

2. Try to use the dirty diaper to wipe up as much of the mess as you can before you break out the clean cloths or wipes.

3. During the first month, it might work best to wipe your baby's butt with plain water (except in the case of the tarry meconium mentioned earlier). You can use an infant washcloth, cut-up towel, soft paper towel, or cotton balls. Commercial baby wipes can irritate the wild newborn's skin, so check how your infant's skin responds to them before going all out. You can find sensitive wipes that might help the situation.

4. For a female wild infant, you should wipe front to back, using a clean section of the washcloth or cotton each time. This is to avoid spreading poop to the vagina, which can cause infection. For a boy, throw an extra diaper over the penis while cleaning, to reduce the chances of the squirt-gun effect.

5. Once the diaper is changed, put the wild infant down in a safe place and dump any poop you can from the dirty diaper into the toilet (this goes for both cloth and disposable diapers). When you've done this, wash your hands thoroughly.

Changing diapers becomes more challenging as the wild infant gains independence and is able to kick your hands, flip over, stand up, or do black-belt karate on you. If the situation gets downright dangerous, you might have to change the location of the diapering to a washable rug on the floor. Once your baby is able to stand up, you might have to change the diaper as he stands. Once your baby is able to get in the car and drive away from your attempts to change him, he shouldn't be wearing a diaper, now, should he?

SUPER DIAPER TIPS

Once you've got the basic technique of diapering down pat, you can apply these tips to make the job even easier and smoother.

- ❧ Prepare—Get all your diapering gear together *before* you open that soiled surprise your infant is wearing. Once you open it, you'll need to deal with a lot of things at once, while trying not to puke. So it's good to have your stuff ready. "Ready" means within arm's reach so you don't have to leave the filthy specimen.

- ❧ Watch for Pinching—If you have a changing table with a strap, slide your hand between your baby's belly and the clip before fastening it, so you don't pinch your baby's oh-so-soft skin. Pinching a wild infant is not a good way to get started on this.

- ❧ Speed Bonus!—Try to change the diaper as quickly as you can. The faster you can clean and change the little human, the happier everyone will be.

- ❧ But Be Accurate—Having said that about speed, you should also be totally precise. If you don't line up the new diaper properly, you'll only be facing future leakage and/ or a cranky baby. So, just be super fast and brain surgery– accurate, is all. No biggie, right?

- ❧ Shield Yourself—Put a washcloth or spare cloth diaper under infants of either gender, and for male wild infants, place another one over his wee-wee while changing. He has no idea he's not supposed to pee when the diaper's off! Ready, aim, fire! Newborns are especially susceptible to the diaper-free peeing.

- ❧ Let It Go—If you have one of those super wild and crazy active infants, you might need to give up on the idea of using a changing table. Diapering on the run is a very impressive skill to acquire, and you will have some awesome stories to tell at parties. But not at dinner parties. Actually, maybe not at any parties.

THE WILD CARD: DIAPER RASH

If there's anything that can make a wild infant's diaper change more challenging than it already is, it's diaper rash. This common situation, which ranges from mild redness to bleeding sores, can make your wild infant exponentially more wriggly, screechy, and miserable.

Here is some basic information to know ahead of time:

❖ **Some babies get frequent diaper rash, while others hardly ever get it. Diaper rash occurs most commonly when babies begin to eat solid foods, when they sleep through the night in a dirty diaper, and when they are taking antibiotics.**

❖ **To help get rid of diaper rash, change diapers frequently, and expose your wild infant's butt to some air and light. In a warm room, put her belly down on a disposable absorbent pad or use a waterproof crib pad with a cloth diaper on top. Don't leave her alone. Once again, make sure that the wild infant does not think it is appropriate to air out her butt in adulthood. Once she's walking, you can let her run wild and naked through the house to air out any rashy skin, but be prepared for her to pee on the floor. Your friendly little pet dog will *not* lick that spill. Or worse—maybe he will.**

❖ **There is no need to slather ointment on your wild infant during every diaper change to prevent rash. But if you see the first signs of diaper rash (slight redness) you should start treating it right away. It won't go away on its own, and most likely it will worsen and become very irritating to your poor little infant. If left untreated, a simple case of diaper rash can become a yeast infection, which is much harder to treat than regular diaper rash. Nobody wants to have their first yeast infection before they're even a year old.**

- The AAP recommends that you not use any baby powders. Strange, right, considering how our adult human mothers dumped that stuff all over our butts! Apparently though, if baby powder is inhaled, it can cause breathing problems and lung damage. If you do decide to use a powder, use a cornstarch-based type. You will want to use it sparingly, shaking it into your hand away from the baby. Don't allow the powder to build up in your infant's neck or groin folds.

A Rash Decision

If the "run naked and free" approach is not a suitable option or doesn't fully clear up the rash on your wild infant, you may need to use ointments. These are usually oil-based (such as Vaseline, A+D Ointment, or plain olive oil), or zinc oxide–based (such as Desitin or Balmex). These ointments create a barrier to protect the wild infant's skin, and have to be spread on thickly to work. You can also find a wide variety of other brands and types, including organic and all-natural varieties. Here are some more tips about soothing your untamed infant's wild diaper rash:

- **Think Outside the Species**—We know your wild infant is a crazy little mammal, but should you use ointments meant for other animals? Some human moms say yes. It's not uncommon to use Bag Balm, which is meant for cows with chapped udders. The infant will probably end up drinking cow's milk anyway, so she may as well use her balm, too. And hey, maybe you can try that stuff on your udders.
- **Thin Skin?**—Don't use over-the-counter hydrocortisone cream unless you've discussed it with the doctor. This can thin an untamed infant's skin, and their skin is pretty thin in the first place.

- **Yeast Infections**—If you think your wild one might have a yeast infection, don't break out the Vagisil—call the pediatrician. He or she might prescribe an anti-fungal cream like Lotrimin or a combination steroid/antifungal cream like Lotrisone. Be sure not to use prescription ointments any longer than prescribed. Using this as a regular diaper cream can lead to serious side effects in kids, including thinning of the skin. We've all known (and probably worked with) a person with thin skin, and do you really want your kid to grow up to be that guy?

- **Cocoa Butter**—People in humid climates like Hawaii use pure cocoa butter as diaper rash prevention. It's available in most drugstores as solid bars or sticks that need to be warmed up. (Not like microwave warmed, like put-in-a-bowl-of-warm-water or sunny-windowsill warmed.) Test it on your own skin to be sure it's not too hot before you put it on the wild infant.

- **Plantain Leaves**—If you happen to live near a grocery store that sells goods for a Latino community, you might be able to find another natural remedy for diaper rash—plantain leaves. Crush the fresh leaves and use them to line the diaper of your wild infant. But remember this when you find them later, so you don't wonder why your baby is pooping leaves.

- **Vinegar**—If you're dealing with diaper rash and you wash your diapers at home, try adding vinegar to your rinse water. Or you can add vinegar to your baby's bath water, using about one cup of white vinegar in a normal tub, or less than one-third cup in a sink or baby tub. Urine is irritating because it's alkaline, and the acid in vinegar can reduce the alkalinity. Urine is also irritating because it's gross and smells bad.

🐾 **Wiped Out**—Skip the diaper wipes while your baby has a rash. While your baby is rashy, diaper wipes—even those for sensitive skin—might only make the rash worse. Stick to a soft cloth and plain water.

Chapter 8

THE FOOD CHAIN

By the time you finally get used to feeding your baby whatever liquid you've chosen—and dealing with the ensuing diapers—guess what? It might just be time to start offering solid foods to the ravenous wild infant. The fully-grown human generally crushes and grinds solid food with a set of thirty-two strong, prey-devouring tusks. Your wild infant might have begun to grow the infant equivalent of these, and it is your job to approach his open jaws with meager offerings of puréed delights. Be careful—he doesn't know that teeth hurt when fastened onto flesh!

DON'T PANIC

If all of this talk makes you a little bit nervous, don't worry. The fact is, solid food is actually considered a "supplement" during an untamed infant's first year. The main dish is still that good old liquid you've been providing. So don't feel like you have to rush! Look, some people live on Slim-Fast, don't they?

Here are some great reasons why it's okay to hold off on solid foods for up to eight months. After eight months, though, you're gonna want to pass the potatoes, dude. That kid is hungry!

WHAT THE INFANT'S BODY DOES TO GET READY

At around six months, the wild *Kingdomius infantius* specimen's body begins to undergo changes that are specifically designed for the eating of solid foods. For example, it marks the end of the untamed infant's tongue extrusion reflex, which causes things that go in the baby's mouth to be pushed out with her tongue. Feeding solids will be much easier if the food is not being immediately shoved out of the mouth onto your lap, don't you think?

Note: Some clever infants may grow into kids who try to pull the old "tongue extrusion reflex" excuse on you later. Do not believe your child when she's five and insists she can't eat her Brussels sprouts because her tongue is involuntarily pushing them out. Nice try, kid. Why does that never happen when you're eating ice cream?

In addition, around six or eight months, the untamed baby's intestines begin secreting a protein known as immunoglobulin A (IgA), which prevents allergens from passing into the bloodstream. Giving a baby solid foods before this defense is in place will likely result in your wild infant turning into a little gastrointestinal mess. And for infants, allergies and intolerances often equal "nasty poop."

BEFORE YOU RUSH IN ◇ ◇ ◇

Take a minute and think about what solid food will do to your life on the diaper end of infant care. Solid food will quickly transform that liquidy, relatively innocuous breastmilk poop into what looks like bobcat feces. Seriously, once a person is eating actual food, poop becomes—well, actual poop. And you are the one who's going to be cleaning that stuff up. Unless you have some really weird fetishes, I see no reason why you'd be rushing into that. Likewise, spit-up is more likely to be "chunky style."

WHEN WILL SHE BE READY FOR SOLIDS?

Of course, some wild infants have to go and be ahead-of-the-curve overachievers, even when it comes to chewing and digesting nonliquid nutrition. For whatever reason, these wild infants are just dying to try those puréed organic peas before the other kids do. Wow, you've got a real Foodie Howser, MD!

Having a precocious chewer is just about the only situation where it makes sense to start feeding solids ahead of schedule. Experts say you should start your untamed infant on solids only if he is at least four months old and is acting as if he's going to start eating solid foods with or without you.

Here are a few signs your wild infant might be ready for solids:

🐾 He stares obsessively at you and your human partner while you eat your meals, or maybe he grabs your food and tries to shove it in his mouth.

🐾 He tries to "chew" on all of his toys (or has devoured several of them).

🐾 He drinks a ton of breastmilk and then eats your breasts.

🐾 He secretly calls and orders pizza for delivery.

🐾 He sits up with support, and is able to control his head well enough to lean forward when he wants more food.

🐾 He is able to control your head when he wants more food.

🐾 He drinks more than thirty-two ounces of formula, or breastfeeds six or seven times a day, and wants more.

🐾 He is at least twice his birth weight, or at least 13 to 15 pounds.

🐾 He is larger than either you or your partner, and seems ready to eat both of you, as well as the entire town you live in, if you don't offer him some instant rice cereal now.

🐾 He's started chewing gum to suppress his appetite.

🐾 His favorite song is the Chili's "baby back ribs" jingle.

BABY'S FIRST APPETIZER: RICE CEREAL

Once you have determined that your wild infant is prepared to ingest solid foods, the next step is to figure out what to give this insatiably hungry little beast. You can't just throw him your leftover pizza and say, "Go for it, kid." In the beginning, you have to start out slow, and feed the wild baby something he can handle. Remember, this whole eating thing is still very new to him.

Store-Bought Rice Cereal

The first semi-solid food you will want to feed your wild infant will probably be rice cereal. Although it's not exactly a gourmet meal, you can't be too worried about that in the beginning. Rice cereal is easy to digest and unlikely to cause an allergic reaction.

GO WITH THE FLOW

If your untamed baby is prone to constipation, you can replace rice with a barley- or oat-based cereal instead. Because your feral creature may still be vulnerable to food allergies, wheat probably isn't the best idea at the beginning.

Worried about how in the world you are going to whip up a delicious and nutritious bowl of baby cereal? Worry no more! You can get rice cereal in instant, ready-to-mix brands at the grocery store, usually labeled "baby cereal" or "wild infant feed" or something of the like.

To prepare the instant cereal, mix about two teaspoons of the cereal with formula or breastmilk (or, if the cereal includes powdered formula, just add water). You can vary the texture to find out what your untamed baby likes best, but you should start a little more on the watery side.

Making It Yourself

Of course, if you are obsessed with feeding your infant homemade everything, you can go ahead and make your own rice cereal from scratch. This is great for people who have a whole lot of extra time. You can make a simple rice cereal by cooking rice and water into a mush, or you can use a fancier recipe if you have one. Your wild infant will be a little food snob in no time!

Keep in mind that unlike instant cereals, homemade rice cereals aren't fortified with iron, and at around the time most wild infants start eating solids (six months), they are also ready for an iron boost in their diets. Ask your pediatrician if your hungry little creature needs the additional iron. If he does need iron, you're probably better off with the instant cereal. (If you have the kind of free time that allows you to fortify your own homemade cereal with iron, I'd like to invite you to come over and feed my baby, too.)

THE GEAR

If you haven't caught on to this by now, caring for a wild infant means needing a ridiculous amount of supplies and accessories for each of the tiny creature's needs and functions. Feeding solid foods is certainly no exception. Be prepared for your wild infant's first feedings to be about as messy as you can possibly imagine. These creatures are truly wild, and they have absolutely no notion of table manners. For a while, you're just going to need to accept that your home is going to look like a prison food fight. Unless you've got a family dog, who might gobble up the little slob's spillage.

Here are some of the helpful items you will want to have on hand when your untamed little eater is ready to tear into some solids:

- Infant feeding spoon or demitasse spoon (those little spoons used for cappuccino). But definitely do not give that wild creature any cappuccino; that is the last thing this little mayhem-maker needs
- Big bibs for the wild infant; even bigger bib (or apron, if you want to act like a "grownup") for you
- Sturdy high chair with safety strap, or infant seat
- Plastic cups, both with and without tops, ideally with handles; "no-spill" cups
- Food processor, blender, or food grinder (if you plan to make baby food yourself)
- Washcloths (lots of 'em!)
- Disposable self-stick placemats or washable high chair trays
- A plastic mat, towel, or dog to catch spills under the high chair

THE FIRST SUPPER

The time to try the first "real" feeding of your wild infant is when she seems hungry, but not ravenously, could-eat-a-horse hungry. Don't worry about sitting her in her high chair if you don't have it set up yet; all that novelty might overwhelm her. The first few solid-food dinners are kind of like "eating practice" until she gets the whole thing figured out. And don't worry, she will. If there's one thing just about all humans eventually get very good at, it's eating. Some of us get way, way *too* good at it.

Here are a few steps to braving those first few encounters with solid foods. Good luck!

1. **If you're not using a high chair, put your untamed baby in an infant seat, or in the lap of an available and reliable adult. Make sure she is sitting mostly upright, with her head tipped ever so slightly back.**

2. Scoop a small bit of cereal on the spoon, or your own finger if that works better, and put it just into the front of the wild baby's mouth. Do *not* shove the food into her mouth. The idea of "eating practice" is for her to learn how to get the food off the spoon and far enough into her mouth to swallow it. Don't worry too much—wild infants at this stage usually love putting everything in their mouths. Just present the spoon, and she will probably put it in her mouth without thinking twice.

3. Here's the hard part, especially if you are a bit of a control freak. Once you present the spoon of cereal, you have to let the wild creature do whatever she wants with that cereal, barring slipping poison into it and feeding it back to you. For example, she might try to suck the spoon. She might try to use her spoon as a slingshot and fire the rice cereal into your face. She might shove the cereal out with her tongue. Just patiently scoop the cereal off her chin and back into her mouth.

4. Don't pressure her in any way. She might eventually swallow the cereal, and then open her mouth for more. Give her as many spoonfuls of cereal as she wants. But once she turns away, she's done. Don't try to talk her into taking another bite. Let it be a new, interesting experience for her, and stop when she stops.

5. If she starts to get bored and you can tell she's probably not going to keep eating, wipe her off and put the food and food gear away. Bring it out the next day at about the same time. If she flips out and rejects the food— screaming, closing her mouth against it, etc.—try it again the next day. If she rejects the food several days in a row, ask her what's up with the hunger strike. Maybe she's protesting something. If she doesn't seem to be a

political activist, maybe she's just not ready for solids yet. Try again in a few weeks.

6. Remember, your wild infant might be manipulative at this age, but she isn't really all that bright. So use your intellectual advantage to trick her. She might try to play with her food, or mush up the cereal with her fingers. It might feel counterintuitive, but let her. She'll probably end up licking the food off her fingers—mission accomplished. Or she might refuse to open her mouth, so how about *you* take a bite of this scrumptious rice cereal? And remember to lie about how delicious it is!

SKIP THE BOTTLES

Don't put solid foods in a bottle or infant feeder unless the doctor has instructed you to. For one thing, it's a lot easier to overfeed a baby this way. For another thing, the whole idea of this is to get used to solids, so why serve it as a liquid?

INTRODUCING THE SECOND FOOD

Once you get your wild infant chowing down on the rice cereal pretty consistently, you should keep that as the main dish for two weeks to a month. You can try to give it a little "variety" by preparing it with a thicker consistency as your ravenous creature sharpens his eating skills.

At some point, your untamed infant might be like, "OMG, can we *please* have something for dinner besides rice cereal? If I have that one more time I am seriously gonna throw up in my mouth using my tongue extrusion reflex!"

When your baby is ready to transition to second foods, start introducing new foods slowly. Like, very slowly. Sorry, baby, your diet doesn't get to be exciting yet. But just be thankful it's not 24/7 rice cereal.

What Should I Serve?

There are mixed opinions on what is a good "second" food (everyone pretty much loves rice cereal as food No. 1). Some say that the second food should be vegetables rather than fruits, so that the wild infant does not expect all foods to be sweet. However, others think because fruits are sweet, they are a good way to get kids interested in eating. Basically, you should go with whatever seems to be working best for your baby, and whatever makes sense to you.

Be careful not to impose your ideas about food onto your poor little wild infant. Don't steer away from avocado because you think it's icky, and don't load the poor kid up on sweet potatoes because you love them. If anything, you should act like you love the foods you don't love, so your wild infant can think he's rebelling against you.

These are the top ten second foods for wild infants. Choose among them based on your little chewer's reaction and preferences.

- 🐾 Peas
- 🐾 Sweet potatoes
- 🐾 Squash
- 🐾 Pears
- 🐾 Avocado
- 🐾 Bananas
- 🐾 Applesauce
- 🐾 Barley cereal
- 🐾 Oat cereal
- 🐾 Rice cereal

Go Slooooooowly

Did I mention that? Feed your wild infant a single new food, in teensy portions, for at least three days straight before adding another food. When you give the wild baby a new food, keep an eye out for allergic reaction or intolerance. This is a great time to study your wild infant's reactions to food and learn about food intolerances and allergies. If all the little guy has had for three days is peas, and he's sneezing and rash-covered, you have good reason to think he might have a problem with peas.

To help you remember what you served and how your wild infant reacted, keep a chart of the foods you have introduced to the wild infant, and note any reactions the little gobbler has had.

MAKING YOUR OWN BABY FOOD

In recent years, more wild infant parents have begun making their own baby food. As a result, some parents might look at you in total horror if you do not have the time or the inclination to purée and freeze your own wild infant food. They will say, "Ohhh . . . I see—you use food from the *jar*?" Be aware that the tone these parents use when they say "from the jar" will make it sound like you extracted the baby food from the nearest sewer. However, you should not feel guilty about this, or feel pressured to set up a baby food factory in your home. Babies generally only eat mushed-up foods for a few months, anyway; then they zip right on to finger foods. So do what works best for your family.

However, if you do decide to whip up a batch of wild infant food, it's actually pretty easy. You can make some and then freeze it for later. Here are some tips:

🐾 **Buy fresh vegetables and fruits and use them within a day or two so they don't go bad. Whatever you think about Gerber, at least they don't sell "puréed rotten bananas."**

🐾 **Peel the fresh fruits or veggies, remove any seeds or cores, then steam or boil until soft. Note: Bananas don't need to be cooked, since they're already pretty soft and mashable.**

🐾 **Purée the mixture well, using a blender, a food processor, or a baby food grinder. There's one called the Baby Bullet, but do not encourage your infant to take up firearms.**

🐾 **Freeze individual portions in ice cube trays. You can then take the cubes out of the trays and store them, in bags in the freezer. Note: Make sure you label and date the bags.**

Note # 2: Do not accidentally put a puréed fish ice cube in your glass of iced tea. That is really not a good taste.

🐾 Be sure to use the frozen portions in time. Frozen fruit and veggie purées are good for three months, while puréed fish, meat, and chicken are good for up to eight weeks. Note: A rotten fish ice cube is even worse in your iced tea glass. Just don't try it, is all I'm saying.

🐾 You can defrost the little food cubes in the microwave, but just until barely warm. As with a bottle of microwaved formula, you will want to stir the food thoroughly to avoid "hot spots." You can thin the purée using breastmilk, formula, or water. Avoid butter, oil, sugar, or salt.

🐾 While you are still testing new foods for allergic reactions, it is better not to get too fancy with mixing while making your purées. As creative as "puréed pears and beef" might sound, you'll be adding to your confusion if your child should have a reaction to the dish—you won't know which ingredient was the problem. Once you have exposed your child to each individual ingredient and are pretty sure he's not allergic, mix away.

Is It Organic?

We all have seen the label "organic" placed on any number of food products for infants, kids, adults, dogs, cats, you name it. And wild creatures pretty much subsist on organic matter, except for maybe raccoons, who would probably eat dirty sports bras if they could. Of course you want to give your child healthy food, but how do you know whether the stuff you buy really lives up to the claim and is worth the extra money?

Don't just take fancy labels at their word—just because a food says it is "organic" or "wholesome" or, vaguest of all, "natural," that doesn't mean much. Remember, hurricanes and syphilis are natural.

Let's take a closer look at some of the ins and outs of organic baby food.

The Good Ol' USDA

Only baby food that carries the label "USDA Organic" has met the official criteria established by the United States Department of Agriculture. So look for that on any baby food label while shopping for some peace of mind. If your own homemade food doesn't have this label, you need to ask yourself some tough questions about your product. Don't go easy on you!

In order to acquire the "USDA Organic" label, a food has to be at least 95 percent organic. This means that all but 5 percent of the dish was made without conventional fertilizers or pesticides. Organic food also can't be genetically modified, produced with hormones or antibiotics, or exposed to radiation. Regarding the remaining 5 percent of the food, well, that's the best the USDA can give you at this point.

Making Your Own Organic Baby Food

If you're making your own wild infant food and want to go organic, choose fruits and vegetables that also carry the "USDA Organic" label. Also, quit injecting the ingredients with antibiotics, stop using pesticides in your recipes, and for the love of God, step away from those hormones you're dying to dump into your food processor. Look, I know all of this stuff is delicious! I personally love a pesticide-and-estrogen sandwich! But you want organic food, right?

Buying Store-Bought Organic Baby Food

Jarred organic food is more expensive, but you can save money by buying in bulk or looking for sales. Your wild infant will show his appreciation for your effort by spitting the organic food up on you in a vigorous, very healthy way.

SAFETY TIPS FOR FEEDING THE WILD INFANT

Just as you'd be careful if you were, say, feeding a ravenous lion some fresh hyena carcass, you might be inclined to tread carefully when approaching the cavernous jaws of your wild infant. But don't worry too much—although your infant might be perfectly willing to devour your feeding hand, she isn't quite fast or strong enough to achieve this (yet). Luckily, by the time she is in top parent-eating form, she will have acquired a little something called *empathy*. So, you see, it all works out. Really!

Right now, the main thing you should be careful about is keeping the infant food safe and fresh. Here are some pointers for this:

- **Don't feed the wild infant directly from the jar. Once saliva enzymes from that cute little demitasse spoon touch the food, they break down nutrients and speed up the spoiling process. To avoid causing the food to go bad from drool enzymes, put a meal's worth of food into a bowl and serve from that. If for whatever reason you have to feed from the jar, throw the leftovers away.**
- **Refrigerate unused food immediately. Also, don't drool or spit all over it, as per the previous instruction.**
- **Don't keep an open, refrigerated jar of baby food longer than two days. Even if it tastes A-okay to you, it could contain unseen bacteria that might harm your wild infant. Don't eat it yourself, either; I'm not sure if this same bacteria can hurt you, but do you really want to start eating baby food?**
- **If you give your baby canned food and you use a can opener, you should use a can opener designated specifically for this. For example, don't use the same can opener you use to open the dog's food. And hey, isn't the dog getting pretty full on baby food spills?**
- **Once your baby starts drinking juice, only give him pasteurized juices. Why? Because I said so, okay?**

JUNGLE
PLAYDATE

Hey, don't you call my mama a pig! A strange—but hardly new—area of scientific research called reproductive ectogenesis focuses on the use of artificial wombs to incubate an embryo. One such concept proposes using pigs as surrogate mothers for human infants. This idea, first discussed as early as 1932, was proposed in 1984 as an alternative to abortion. Human embryos destined for abortion would instead be transplanted into a transgenic pig, which would gestate the baby to term. The infant would then be placed in an adoptive home. This idea has been pretty slow to catch on due to the obvious ethical issues. However, a 2011 survey conducted at Arizona State University found that 41 percent of survey respondents would support such technology. The whole thing could get pretty confusing, though, if a baby gestated in this way grew up to eat the pig who gestated him. That's not right—show some respect for your mom!

- -

MEAT AND DAIRY

Although meat and dairy might eventually become a staple of your wild creature's diet in childhood, babies usually don't start eating meat until about eight months of age. At about this age, you can start giving him a taste of puréed meat.

Don't be too surprised or upset if those little jars of pinkish-grayish puréed meat aren't overly appetizing to your wild infant. Take a good look at that stuff. Would you eat it?

If your infant rejects the lovely helping of "ham and gravy" that looks like Silly Putty, don't stress. You can always try to mix meats with puréed veggies, or grind up meats from your own dinner, which might have more flavor than jarred versions. Or you can just wait until he can pick up that first little bit of a chicken finger and go to town himself. Remember, in the first year, meat isn't even necessary. Your little creature is getting sufficient protein from formula or breastmilk.

As for dairy, wait until your wild infant is at least a year old before giving him dairy products. You might find that surprising, since he's been drinking breastmilk or formula all this time. However, cow's milk is different—it contains a protein that's not so easy for a baby's digestive system to break down. For you, this equals nasty diarrhea. Unless you just can't wait for that, hold off on the dairy.

VEGETARIAN/VEGAN DIET

You and your adult human partner might have decided that your wild infant will follow a vegetarian or vegan diet, like a cute little wild granola cruncher. (Granola is way too difficult to chew and is a choking hazard for a wild infant, so I mean this in a figurative sense only.)

Vegetarian and vegan diets, if handled responsibly and carefully, can supply adequate nutrition to a growing wild infant.

Sure, your wild infant might decide to experiment with meat later on (if you catch your wild infant in your backyard trying to hunt a squirrel, maybe she's trying to tell you she likes meat). But it's not her decision right now. She can't even choose her outfits yet, so she can just wear those little Birkenstocks you got her and love them!

Here's some information on feeding your wild infant a vegetarian or vegan diet:

- A vegetarian diet that includes milk and eggs can easily meet your wild infant's nutritional needs. Talk to your infant's pediatrician about how to incorporate this diet during these early feedings.
- A vegetarian diet should include lots of iron-rich foods, such as stewed dried fruits, beans, and iron-fortified cereal. You might also give the untamed vegetarian a daily multivitamin with iron; ask the pediatrician.
- Your wild infant needs quite a bit of fat and calories before the age of two. At this time, fat and calories go toward brain development. Later on, in adulthood, the brain quits developing and the calories and fat go toward rapid thigh and butt development. (No, of course it's not fair. What is fair in this life?) Make sure your infant gets plenty of calories and fat by giving him foods like mashed avocado, vegetable oil, and nut and seed butters.
- A vegan diet (no eggs, dairy, or food derived from animals) is definitely more challenging for a wild infant. Some vitamins, such as vitamin B12, vitamin D, and riboflavin, are mainly found in animal products. Again, talk to your pediatrician about how to work this out.

ALLERGIC REACTIONS AND INTOLERANCES

When you're slowly introducing early foods to your wild infant, you can study the strange little fellow to see if he is having any strange reactions to any of these food items. If your baby has some of the milder symptoms, you can try putting that food on hold for a while, and giving it another try in a few months. Wheezing and rashes, though, are more serious, so call the doctor right away. Your child's pediatrician can help you determine whether this food should be eliminated permanently.

Here are some of the symptoms of a possible allergic reaction or food intolerance:

- Skin reactions: rashes on the face or torso, severe diaper rash, hives, eczema
- Digestive problems: vomiting, diarrhea, gas
- Swollen lips or eyelids
- Crankiness
- Stuffed nose

PEANUTS

The American Academy of Pediatrics recommends that untamed children at higher risk of developing food allergies not eat peanut butter until they are three years old. Your wild infant would be considered at "higher risk" if you or a family member has food allergies, asthma, eczema, or hay fever.

If you do decide to give your wild toddler some peanut butter, keep in mind that despite the sharpness of their little teeth, young kids have not yet perfected the art of eating. One thing they really enjoy is swallowing without chewing, and sticky foods like peanut butter can become a choking hazard. To avoid this issue, spread the peanut butter thinly on a cracker or bread, and don't serve the peanut butter in "dollops." In fact, dollops of anything are probably a bad idea during the "swallow without chewing" phase. You should also make sure that your child is seated while eating, and that there is an adult human overseeing the peanut butter—eating maneuver.

READ THE LABELS

Although later in life you might encourage your wild creature to avoid unfair "labels" when it comes to other people, labels are great when it comes to puréed plums or strained peaches. You just can't take those foods at their word—they might contain extra sugar and/or thickeners to appeal to your wild infant's sweet tooth (or, as the case may be, sweet gums). The logic behind this is that wild infants enjoy yummy, sweet foods. This is true, but wild infants also enjoy throwing food at your face, peeing like a loaded squirt gun, and pulling your hair out in clumps for entertainment. This does not mean you should accommodate these pastimes.

Not too long ago, the press made a bit of a fuss about additives in baby foods, so the manufacturers have been somewhat forced into behaving. However, they might still try to sneak in some uncool ingredients using other names. Here are some of the aliases for "sugar" or "bright happy colors that do not exist in nature":

🐾 **Too Sweet—Be on the lookout for words like fructose, dextrose, or maltodextrins. These are all sugars masquerading as something scientific and boring. The companies are hoping your eyes will glaze over and you won't even finish reading these long, annoying words. If they wrote, "sugar, sugar, sugar, and more sugar," you might put that jar down.**

🐾 **Too Corny—Corn products, such as corn syrup for sweetness and cornstarch for thickening, can prompt the very sensitive allergic tendencies of a wild newborn. Not to mention the ongoing controversy about high-fructose corn syrup and its possible links to obesity and other sorts of health problems. You probably don't want to get your wild baby hooked on corn syrup before he's even a fully independent chewer.**

🐾 **Artificial Flavors and Colors—Really, this wild infant food-making stuff can and should be simple. If you're going to manufacture puréed plums, just put the plums** in the food processor and serve it up. When baby food makers feel the need to add artificial colors to their products, such as Red No. 40, Yellow No. 5, etc., you almost have to wonder what was so cosmetically wrong with the original food. It's not as though wild infants even know what color foods are supposed to be. However, you do. And now you also know that numbered colors are totally avoidable.

DRINKING PRACTICE

At about the same time you are trying out solids with your wild infant, you can also start teaching her to drink from a cup. Yes, that's right—your little creature is going to be learning a lot of stuff all at once. Luckily, she won't have to worry about potty training for a while yet. Whew. Things will be stressful for her, what with all that drinking and eating, but at least she can still pee and poop her pants whenever she wants. That's a great plus.

Anyway, you can start with "drinking practice" at about five months. Of course, for some of us, "drinking practice" continues throughout life, almost as though we're planning to compete at an Olympic level.

Types of Cups

Your wild infant will need to learn how to use the three different kinds of infant cups: those without a top, those with a spouted lid, and no-spill cups. The different cup types offer different levels and speeds of flow. Your wild infant needs to be able to control the flow of liquids with her lips. Some human beings struggle their whole lives with "controlling the flow of liquid to their lips," so to speak, so be patient with your little creature. This is a tough lesson!

1. No-spill or "sippy" cups have valves inside their lids, and drinking from them is similar to drinking from a bottle. These are what you're likely to start out with, since she is already familiar with sucking. They're also by far the cleanest option of the three.

2. Spouted lid cups allow the stuff to come out in a small stream, and are good for drinking with finger foods. He won't have to work as hard as he did with a no-spill cup, but the cup still has a top.

3. No-top cups obviously offer a free flow of juice or milk. These are good for initial practice, and then probably not until your infant is much more adept at holding the cup himself without sloshing the liquid all over the place. He'll also need to be able to manage how much comes out with each sip. Have your spill-slurping dog at the ready!

Once your wild infant is able to achieve all kinds of sips with her little lips, she will be on her way to becoming an expert drinker! Congratulations!

Drinking 101 for Wild Infants

Though your wild infant will likely enjoy banging the cup around more than trying to drink from it, here are some tips for getting the liquid into the infant mouth:

🐾 Start with "practice" sips of breastmilk, formula, or water from a cup. You can also offer her a small swig from your cup of water, by putting the cup to her lips and tipping it so just a teensy dribble comes out. This is very likely to be a total failure, and will end up trickling down her chin. That's okay. You are introducing her to the concept. If at first you don't succeed . . . do another load of laundry. Sadly, your roving vacuum dog will probably have very little interest in cleaning up spilled water.

- Because these first attempts will probably be seriously messy, you should try this either at bathtime, mealtime, or when you're preparing to change her clothes. Be patient, and remember you're just starting out.

- Once your untamed offspring has begun eating solids, drinking from a cup might become more of a serious affair. You can allow her to have small amounts of juice to go with her big-girl solids. You should probably water the juice down, though, so she doesn't get too full from juice alone. Try to keep the actual juice content at less than four ounces per day. Don't be too specific in teaching her how to water stuff down, though—you don't want her to apply that trick to your liquor cabinet in seventeen or so years.

Finger Food!

Once your untamed baby reaches the age of between eight and ten months, he will be the king of slurping and swallowing. He will have passed his food allergy and intolerance tests with flying colors (and those colors will probably not be Red No. 40). Daily feedings will be a well-oiled machine—you'll serve up a few bowls of rice cereal, a few servings of puréed fruits and veggies, a few sips of watered-down juice. Things will be going great; you'll sort of wish it could stay like this forever. But if there's one thing you will learn as the parent of a wild infant, it's this: just when you think you have it all worked out, the rules will completely change on you. So, if your little mushy mealtimes are starting to seem awesome and well managed, it probably means that phase is about to end. By twelve months, it's very likely that you will have a little self-server on your hands.

The Transition

Here's a little snippet of what you can expect as you and your infant venture bravely into solid food consumption. One day, you'll be going for his favorite strained carrots, breaking out the demitasse spoon like a pro, and when the choo-choo heads toward the tunnel, the "tunnel" abruptly snaps shut. It appears the tunnel is closed indefinitely to the mush train. In other words, your wild infant has had enough goop and gruel. Can you really blame him?

The trouble is, he doesn't really have a full set of teeth yet, and he doesn't really know how to handle a knife and fork. So, now what? One thing you can offer your wild infant is lumpier baby foods. The prepared baby food brands usually marked "Stage Three" are meant for untamed infants who are at that "in between" phase of their eating education. If you are the one making the baby food, leave in some chunks and don't purée them as long. It's possible that the thicker texture and more flavorful taste of these "advanced" baby foods might cause the tunnel to reopen for train traffic. However, don't count on it. If the little guy is stubborn on his "no more mush" stance, he might very well gag on lumpy baby food. Oh, the drama!

Some First Finger Food Options

The trick to giving your wild infant finger foods is to amuse and distract him, teach him to pick up food, and then slip in a spoonful of pears or squash in between. He's practicing his self-feeding skills, but also getting a decent amount of his old mush. The fun new game of picking up finger foods ought to make him more willing to tolerate a bit of glop every so often. Here are some popular first-food choices.

Cheerios

If your ambitious little eater spurns your attempt at lumpy mush, one great approach is to try plain Cheerios or any generic Cheerios knockoff (the kid won't know the difference). Place a few on his high chair tray, and watch him practice his motor skills and eating skills all at once! He will try to pick them up (using the "pincer grasp") and put them in his mouth. This will improve his eye-hand coordination, his chewing and swallowing skills, and maybe even your laundry. Still, though, you should try to slip in some spoonfuls of mush in between Cheerios.

Another plus: Cheerios are made of oats rather than wheat, which is much better for the allergy-prone wild infant. Also, they're "spit soluble" and quickly turn to mush in your baby's mouth.

Teething Biscuit

This is another good "pick-me-up" food that pretty much becomes instant mush in the mouth. Still, though, you should supervise your wild baby while he gums his teething biscuit, since large pieces can still break off and pose a choking hazard. Check labels, since some of these are loaded with sugar!

FINGER-LICKIN' BAD

Some foods that are definitely not suitable for the feral infant to grasp in her opposable thumb and forefinger include whole hot dogs (no, really?), whole grapes, raisins, nuts, seeds, olives, popcorn, potato chips, ice cubes, hard candy, uncooked carrots, and uncooked apples. Honey and eggs are also not recommended until your wild child is about a year old.

Fruits and Vegetables

Many fruits fit all of the criteria of a great finger food—they're soft; they break down into small pieces; and they're easy to swallow. Apples need to be steamed or cooked in the microwave first. Remember to remove any peels or pits, and cut the fruits into baby-sized pieces. Veggies are also great, but you should steam or boil them until they're fairly soft. Boiled vegetables, yum!

Pasta

Now here's some real food! Pasta can be a great early finger food—and a wonderful introduction to carbs—as long as you cook it very soft and choose small shapes. You can serve them plain, with tomato sauce, or with pesto for the discriminating wild baby palate.

Breakfast Foods!

Ah, that lucky baby—based on his finger food needs, he can enjoy the infant equivalent of a Denny's Grand Slam breakfast all day long. Whole-grain waffles (frozen then toasted), pancakes (made from a whole-grain mix and frozen), and French toast (for infants under twelve months, make it with egg yolks only, mixed with formula or breastmilk, just in case of a possible allergic reaction) are excellent finger foods for the pincer grasp beginner. Remember to serve these in very small pieces. You will know when mealtime is over when your wild infant begins using the food more as a paint or sculpture medium than a source of nutrients.

JUNGLE
PLAYDATE

Elephants are all about females rallying around their sisters to raise the kids together. When a baby elephant is born, the ladies of the herd all pitch in—grandmothers, sisters, aunts, even cousins. It's like a big baby shower that never ends. These full-time family babysitters are called "allomothers," and they are involved in every aspect of bringing these calves up right. Where are the dudes? Apparently, they roam free in a bachelor community—isn't that nice? However, according to Jaya Savannah on SacredElephants.com, adolescent boy elephants tend to become aggressive little jerks and break away from the matriarchy. They then go off and find the man-herd, and the adult bulls mentor them in how to keep that testosterone in check.

Chapter 9

GROOMING THE WILD INFANT

Some species of the animal kingdom are born with the innate knowledge of how to groom themselves. If you have a cat species (*Felis catus*) residing in your home, you may have witnessed this. Practically from birth, cats instinctively know how to wash themselves with their tongues, to wipe their faces with their paws, and to hold one leg in the air so that you can have a disturbingly clear view of their butt-cleaning regimen. They just know what to do, pretty much from the word *go*.

The newborn wild infant is nothing like this at all. He has no clue how to do anything.

Lucky for you, the untamed newborn does not become terribly dirty at first, if only for a lack of opportunity. Later on, when he has complicated and colorful foods to soil himself with, or greater mobility to go find some wet paint to roll around in, some bigtime bathing will be in order. But to start, the main goals are to wash his hands, face, neck, and diaper region daily. And, no matter what, do not leave the wild infant alone in the bathtub. This is never, ever safe.

MORE GEAR

As with all things wild infant–related, the grooming of your untamed young will require you to obtain several new accessories.

For the newborn stage, you will only need the basic cleaning tools. However, as the wild infant progresses into older babyhood, she will begin to associate grooming time with various special toys. Interestingly, these toys are frequently designed to resemble other members of the animal kingdom, such as ducks or octopi. These are often very strange ecosystems, since ducks, octopi, and wild infant humans rarely coexist in the same body of water. Indeed, if ever such a meeting took place in nature, it would almost certainly not end well. Nevertheless, these water animal scenarios seem to calm the wild infant.

Anyway, for now, you can stick to the following basic materials:

- Baby bathtub, dishpan, or clean sink
- Giant bath sponge—For the infant to lie on if you don't have an infant tub (if you do not have a giant sponge, you can use another towel)
- Cotton balls—Used for cleaning the eyes and ears of the wild infant
- Plastic cup or spray bottle for rinsing
- Soft brush
- Baby washcloths—For washing, play, and keeping the infant warm
- Baby soap, glycerin bar soap, or "no-tears" shampoo (Warning: despite the "no tears" guarantee, wild infants have been known to cry during hair-washings)
- Foam pad to kneel on when bathing the wild infant in an adult tub (to spare your knees, not to worship your wild infant)
- Nonskid mat—For when the wild infant is ready for a larger body of water (adult tub)
- Foam faucet cover (again, for the adult tub)

SPONGE BATHS

Some parents of wild infants like to start out gradually, by giving their little creature a sponge bath. This is a good way of getting your offspring clean without having to immerse him in a tub just yet. Many newborns aren't big fans of being cold, wet, poked, and prodded, so a sponge bath is a good compromise. And if you think about it, a sponge bath is probably the closest thing to the grooming practices of other animals, except maybe fish (or sea sponges).

The first thing you need to figure out is where you are going to do this sponge bath. A counter next to a sink is a good choice, since the water source is nearby and the counter is waterproof. First, get an assistant to make sure one of you always has a hand on the baby for safety. Lay down a folded bath towel to place the wild infant on, and have a sponge ready to wash your infant. Here are a few other sponge bath supplies that you should have in arm's reach before you start:

- **Several towels, some to keep him warm and others for drying him**
- **At least two washcloths (just think it through: do you want to use the same cloth that you just used to wipe his butt to wipe his face?)**
- **Cotton balls (or another clean washcloth) to clean his eyes**
- **Baby soap or mild bar soap**
- **A clean diaper**
- **Clean clothes**
- **Diaper rash ointment, if you are using it**
- **A plastic cup**

Once you have your supplies in place and your wild infant more or less ready for his sponge bath, it's time to commence the grooming process.

Follow these instructions for sponge-cleansing your young:

1. **Undress the Infant**—Remove your wild infant's clothing so that he is clad only in the diaper. Use a towel to cover your spawn for warmth. You will be uncovering only the specific piece of infant that you will be washing at the time.

2. **Clean His Eyes**—Wipe inside the corners of your untamed baby's eyes, from inside out, using a clean cotton ball or different corner of the washcloth for each eye. You can use cotton balls to wipe his ear folds, but don't mess with the ear canal. Then go on to wash his limbs and the front of his torso.

3. **Wash His Hair**—To wash the hair of the wild one, wet it with the washcloth, add a bit of soap, and gently massage his entire scalp, even the soft spots. Make sure your baby's head is being supported by one hand, and tip it slightly back over the sink. Using your plastic cup, pour warm water back over his head, taking care not to get it in his eyes. If the little guy does get soap in his eyes, wipe them with plain, warm water. He'll open them once the soap is gone and he's done screaming bloody murder.

4. **Neck Folds**—Pay special attention to the creases around your untamed infant's neck. This area tends to collect gunk in the beginning. It might be skin cells being shed, or it might be dried-up milk/formula spills. Either way, you don't want the other untamed infants calling your newborn "old cruddy-neck," do you?

5. **Diaper Region**—Next, remove that diaper and wash the baby's genitals and rear. If your wild infant is a girl, remember you have to wash from front to back to avoid infection.

6. **Back Wash**—Conclude the grooming ritual by sitting the infant up, leaning him forward on your hand as you would when burping him, and wash his back. He might burp, but you asked for that, didn't you? Check to make sure all soap has been rinsed, and dry him with a clean towel, paying special attention to the ick-collecting neck folds.

7. **Fully dry and redress the child.** Now ask yourself, as you survey the pile of wet towels; the soapy, soaked countertop; and the frazzled baby—wasn't that easy?

Miniature Tub Time

Once you have mastered the sponge bath, you can begin to try grooming the wild infant in a smaller version of a bathtub. This can either be an official baby bathtub, a clean dishpan, or even the sink. (The dishwasher is not considered a good site for a wild infant bath. Infants don't stack well, and tend to break coffee mugs.) It is very unlikely that your wild infant will care which one you choose. However, she probably will know the difference between being all gross and covered with dried food and being clean.

If you choose a baby bathtub, consider putting it up on a counter so you're not constantly bending down.

Follow these instructions for tub-grooming your infant:

🐾 **Gather Your Stuff**—Make sure you have your supplies ready ahead of time—this is a great idea for all wild infant scenarios, really. What's the point of having supplies if they're not ready when you need them?

🐾 **Soften the Bottom**—If the baby bathtub doesn't have an infant sling or support, put something soft in the bottom of the tub, like a towel or a special bath sponge. This will provide a nice, soft surface for the tiny infant butt.

- ❧ **Fill 'Er Up**—Fill the tub with only two or three inches of lukewarm water, and test the temperature on the inside of your wrist or elbow. Also, make sure your hot water heater is at a low setting (about 120°F) to avoid dangerous burns.

- ❧ **Put the Infant In**—When you put your baby into the water, remember that most of her body and all of her face should be well above the surface of the water.

- ❧ **Keep the Infant Warm**—*Kingdomius infantius* specimens lose heat when unclothed, so make sure you keep your wild infant warm. Before the bath, set the temperature of your bathroom to a warm and cozy 75°F. Also, keep the infant warm during the bath by layering the extra washcloths over her stomach and pouring warm water on them. This job can be delegated to your partner or any other human. Although he probably means well, the family dog cannot help out on this one—he lacks the opposable thumbs.

- ❧ **No Phones!**—Do not answer the phone—even your cell phone—while bathing your wild infant. Seriously. Even if your friend is calling to tell you who won *Dancing with the Stars*, you will have to wait. You need to have all eyes and hands focused on bathing your squirmy, slippery, unpredictable infant. Remember, for her, being able to take a bath is the motor-skills equivalent of Ralph Macchio being able to dance a tango.

- ❧ **No Razors**—Remove shaving razors from the bathtub area. Life is not that bad.

- ❧ **Dispense It**—If you didn't buy soap in this format already, put liquid baby soap in a clean soap dispenser for one-handed use.

- ❀ Useful Leftover—Remember the spray bottle the hospital gave you to clean your perineum? And remember how you found out what cleaning your perineum is? Well, now you can use it to rinse your baby's hair. Hooray! Note: If you are the male human, just use the spray bottle your partner got from the hospital. Don't worry about that other stuff or think about it ever, ever again.

- ❀ Spray Hose—You can also get a spray hose that attaches to the tub faucet. This can be used to provide clean rinsing water for your baby, and it also makes hair washing easier to do. Another thing that makes hair washing easier is the fact that your infant hardly has any.

- ❀ Washcloths—Lots of washcloths are fun! Remember, you really can't have too many washcloths. They can be used for the bathing part, or keeping the infant warm, or very basic infant bath games. It's impressive how amusing a washcloth can be at that age. I personally still think washcloths are the most hilarious thing ever, but I'm told some people grow out of that.

- ❀ Gentle Cycle—Your baby's skin is super sensitive, as you may know, so don't rub the infant dry. Pat her dry, gently.

- ❀ Warm Towels—You know how you love warm towels fresh from the dryer? Untamed infants do, too. Except in their case, the definition of "warm" is a little different, because their skin is perfect and soft and unblemished, unlike yours. Let them cool slightly before wrapping your infant up in one.

- ❀ The Graduate—When your infant is about to "graduate" from baby tub to grownup tub, start out by getting her a little cap and gown. Then try putting the baby tub inside of the big-kid tub. This will help her get used to the change.

Another option is to take a bath with your baby. This will spare your back since you won't be bending down, and it will enable you to find time for a bath when you might not otherwise. If you bring toy ducks and octopi into the tub for yourself, you're going to have to share them with your wild infant. That's right, even your favorite rubber ducky—just deal with it. Have another adult present to pass the baby to you when you get into the tub, and for the baby hand-off at the end of the bath.

BIG TUB TIME

Once the untamed infant is able to sit steadily without support (usually sometime after six months), he will be ready to migrate to a larger body of water—i.e., the adult tub. This timing will be fortunate for you, since this is probably also the approximate stage at which your wild infant will start slobbering solid food all over himself. There will definitely be some gunk in his neck folds. Here are a few bathtime tips for the baby tub graduate:

- ❧ **Bath Seats—Baby stores sell bath seats or bath rings for this transitional stage. These are designed to give the feral infant extra support within the larger body of water, but your infant won't stay in one for long. As soon as he gets to the crawling stage (which will happen pretty much once you're used to the sitting-up stage) he is going to want to explore that tub like he is Magellan.**
- ❧ **Stay Put—Even if you use a bath ring or bath seat, you still can never leave your infant alone in the bathtub. Even if he tells you he wants to make a few phone calls in private, do *not* leave him!**

- ❧ Co-Tubbing—One reliable approach is to get in the tub with the untamed creature and support him between your legs. You will need another adult human to hand off the infant to you, and then to receive the baby outside of the tub when the bath is done.
- ❧ Bathmat—The old "towel on the bottom of the tub" thing won't work in a big-kid tub, so you should use a nonskid bathmat. It will be soft to sit on and will stop your infant from sliding all over.

BATH TOYS

As previously stated, the untamed infant usually enters a stage, at around the time he is ready for the big tub, when he likes to surround himself with bath toys. The first bath toys you purchase can be on the simple side, such as the following:

- ❧ Nylon bath puff or washcloth—You can wrap some toys in the cloth and let the untamed infant "unwrap" them.
- ❧ Plastic cups—Let's face it, you're going to need a bazillion plastic cups for just about everything the infant does. Pouring water out of cups *never* gets old.
- ❧ Floating plastic book (sadly, this book is not available in a "floatie" edition), boats, dolls.
- ❧ Sponges, cut into cute shapes—"Cute" is subjective, but for the wild infant, this usually means puppies and seals, not Brad Pitt.
- ❧ Rubber ducky, bath puppet.
- ❧ Siblings—Note: If the wild infant does not have siblings residing in his home already, you should not go out and acquire one simply as a bath toy. You also may not wrap a sibling in a cloth or cut them into cute shapes.

PRIVATE PARTS

As a new human parent, another first for you will be cleaning the private parts of a person who is not you. It's understandable that you might be a little bit freaked out by the little girl or boy parts of this strange creature, but keeping these areas clean can prevent infection. And after you've been changing diapers for a while, you'll find that any squeamishness you had will go away. If you are the female human who pushed a baby out of your own private parts in front of a roomful of people, any body-part shyness you had has probably already gone out the window.

Here are some things to keep in mind about your wild infant's private parts.

Boys

If you are a female human, you probably never cared for a penis before. If you are a male human, you probably never cared for anyone else's penis before. But if your wild infant is of male gender, congratulations! You get to make some huge decisions about someone else's penis.

To Snip or Not to Snip

One of the most important decisions you will be faced with is whether you want your untamed infant to be circumcised. It is possible that the decision might be made for you based on religious or cultural beliefs. If not, it's going to be entirely up to you to decide whether or not you think the little guy's foreskin should be snipped.

Here are some of the advantages of circumcision:

- **Reduced risk of urinary tract infections during the first year of life.**
- **May reduce risk of penis cancer.**
- **May reduce risk of sexually transmitted diseases. Not that any son of yours would catch an STD!**
- **Might be linked to lower incidence of AIDS.**

- 🐾 Easier hygiene for the genital area—hey, there's no need to make it more difficult, is there?
- 🐾 If the father is circumcised, he may want the son to look like him. (Aww, I can totally see the family resemblance! So tiny!)

Of course, there are pros and cons to every issue. Critics of circumcision make these arguments against the procedure:

- 🐾 Painful.
- 🐾 May reduce sexual pleasure and performance (circumcision advocates disagree on this point, but how would they know?).
- 🐾 Is a violation of human rights when performed on an infant, since he is not able to make an informed decision.

Ultimately, though, you should just make the best decision you can, based on the information at hand. Your wild infant will be fine with it—or at any rate, he won't remember it.

Penis Care

Here are some instructions for caring for your untamed infant's tiny manhood in the beginning of his life.

- 🐾 If you need to wash the penis, wipe it with a wet cotton ball, and then pat it dry with a clean cloth diaper. You'll probably receive a tube of sterile petroleum jelly from the hospital if your feral infant was circumcised. For the first few days, squeeze some onto a gauze pad and dab it on the tip of the penis every time you change the diaper. This keeps the penis from sticking to the diaper, which is good if you try to imagine the ripped-Band-Aid feeling of detaching the diaper from the penis. (Ouch!) It probably doesn't need to be said, but you should be very gentle with the wild infant's little wee-wee. It's probably sore!

- ❖ After a few days, you may see a yellowish discharge that forms a crust. This is a normal part of healing after circumcision, along with a few spots of blood. If your wild infant's penis oozes blood, however, you should call the doctor.
- ❖ If your untamed baby is not circumcised, don't pull back his foreskin for cleaning—this can cause bleeding and scarring. Normal bathing is fine!

Girls

If your wild infant is a girl, you won't need to worry about issues such as circumcision or gravity-defying projectile pee. Lucky you! However, there are some things to remember when caring for a baby girl, too. When diapering, make sure to wipe your female baby from front to back; this prevents unpleasant urinary tract or other infections. She'll thank you by not screaming in extreme discomfort.

CARING FOR THE BELLY BUTTON

Your newborn wild infant may be fully out of the womb and living in the new habitat of your home, but she still has one remnant of her former habitat—the umbilical cord stump. This cord used to be the hookup to all the awesome free stuff she got from the host organism, *Maternicus martyrius*, in utero. Although the cord was snipped shortly after birth, there's a stub left over, and it will stay there until it eventually dries up and falls off. This can take as few as two weeks or as long as five weeks to happen. Until then, this area should be handled with care, because it is especially vulnerable to infection. Also, don't let your wild infant convince you to cram food into the cord—those days are over, and besides, it totally doesn't work. Not that I would know from personal experience.

Here are some tips for belly button care:

- ❧ **Keep It Dry**—Keep the belly button dry and clean, and expose it to air as much as possible. This doesn't mean you can't give your baby a bath until it's gone, just that you should not cover the cord area with water until it has dried up completely. Ask your pediatrician about it, since doctors have different views on this. (Oh boy, will there be Belly Button Wars someday?)

- ❧ **Watch for Signs of Infection**—If the cord shows signs of redness or pus, call your pediatrician. In the meantime, don't immerse your infant in water.

- ❧ **Swab It if Directed**—You might be instructed to wipe around the base of the cord with a cotton swab dipped in rubbing alcohol several times a day. (Some pediatricians say not to bother with the alcohol.) Alcohol has the dual function of drying the cord and killing bacteria. Do not let the wild infant talk you into using Jack Daniel's as alcohol. As I stated previously, that cord doesn't even work anymore.

GOOD HAIR DAYS

The hair of the wild infant is a very interesting phenomenon—some untamed babies have heads that seem as bald as a hypoallergenic cat, whereas others are born with more hair than a sheep that's into glam rock. But neither of these situations are exactly as they appear: the "cue ball" baby actually does have some fine, light-colored hair, whereas Baby Big Hair might actually lose all of that stuff within six months. Even more odd, once this initial hair falls out, it might grow back a different color than it originally was. So don't get too attached to that purple hair your wild infant has now—it might turn green.

The technical term for your infant's loss of her first hair is telogen effluvium. A wild baby's hormone levels drop significantly after birth, causing hair to go into a "resting" stage and fall out.

JUNGLE PLAYDATE

You wouldn't think a creature described as looking like a "bloated bratwurst with teeth" would feel entitled to start acting like a pushy diva, would you? But apparently the naked mole rat is blind, so she has no idea she's not a hottie. These guinea pig–like animals are seriously weird— they run backward in the dark, among other "eccentric" behaviors. They also have a "queen" mole rat in each community, and she is the only one who actually gets to breed and have babies. How does she keep the other ladies' paws off the men? She pushes them around like a bully, causing them to secrete stress hormones that make them unable to procreate. All so she is the only one to breed a bunch of fugly new mole rats. Hello, ladies? She's blind and gross. Don't let her stress you out!

- -

Cradle Cap

You might have heard other female humans talking about cradle cap and thought, *I must get one of those cradle caps for my untamed infant. They seem to be all the rage.* Bad news: cradle cap is a bunch of thick, yellow scales that cover your *Kingdomius infantius* specimen's head. Not very chic.

This does not mean that she is transforming into a lizard creature. In fact, it usually goes away on its own. But if it bothers you, rub some baby or olive oil onto the scalp, let it soak for a few hours, then gently scrub the scales away with a baby hairbrush, toothbrush, or nailbrush. Then wash it with a mild shampoo to get the oil out. Bye-bye, dragon baby!

Bald Spots

Your infant might develop a bald spot or two, but it's no big deal. This may be related to how her head rubs against the mattress during sleep. You can remedy this by switching up where you put her down for her nap or at night. For the nap, put her down with her head going toward one end of the crib, and at night, put her down with her head on the opposite end. She will turn her head to look out of the crib, and this will take the pressure off the bald side. Or you could just let her keep the bald spots so her dad doesn't feel so bad about his. Family resemblance again!

Nail Trimming

The issue of nail trimming is one that, for new human parents, tends to be a real, well, nail-biter (sorry, it was right there). Parents get very stressed out at the idea of cutting some part of their wild infant and the possibility of drawing blood.

And yes, it's a very delicate operation. Just know that you will get better the more you do it. And your wild infant will probably forgive you for any accidental cuts. Unless he spends his whole life plotting his revenge and ends up attacking you in your sleep with a giant pair of nail clippers when he's thirty-five. But really, how often does that happen?

Your first step is to choose your tools: clippers or scissors. Here's the lowdown.

Clippers Vs. Scissors

Clippers might seem safer than scissors, but that's not always the case. That's because the blades of baby clippers tend to be hard to slip easily under the infant's nails, increasing the chance of pinching his skin. Ow! You should probably consider using what you usually use on your own nails, since that is what you are more comfortable using. No, you cannot use your teeth.

Some human parents find that their own manicure scissors are less likely to cause bleeding than blunt-tipped clippers designed for infant nails because they're more precise. Less bleeding is good.

How to Do the Actual Cutting

- 🐾 **Be Sneaky**—When you are first starting out on nail trimming, wait until your wild one is in a very deep sleep. Signs of deep sleep are arms and legs that flop when lifted, and hands that are open, not in a fist. Also sleep-talking.
- 🐾 **Be Brave**—Hold the scissors or clippers with one hand and with the other, pull the tip of his finger down away from the nail. At this point, you should have better access to the nail. Keep your anxiety in check—remember, it's okay. This is what years and years of therapy will be for. Now go ahead and cut the nail—cut straight across. If you feel you've left sharp corners, you can always gently file these down later.
- 🐾 **Be Sorry**—If you do cut your wild infant, press on the cut and the bleeding should stop fairly quickly. You can also apply antibiotic first-aid cream, and try to soothe your wild infant, although he might not hear your voice over his indignant shrieks.
- 🐾 **Be a Wimp**—If you absolutely recoil at the idea of trying to cut your infant's nails, you can always "wimp out" for the time being and file them down instead. Sure, it's going to take longer than cutting, but they're so soft in the beginning! They're as pliant as they're ever going to be. Besides, it will spare you—and your infant—the whole "blood and hysteria" possibility.

YOU WILL IMPROVE!

Remember, when it comes to untamed infants, practice makes adequate. Sorry, you will never be perfect. But you will get a lot better at nail clipping, because you're going to be doing a lot of it. In fact, your untamed infant's claws might grow to the point of needing trimming several times per week. The good news? Toenails can be left alone for at least a few weeks! Even if they look seriously funky. It's not like he needs to walk anywhere just yet, right?

Chapter 10

YOUR BABY'S JAWS

Well, let's review some of the things we have learned about your wild infant. He is completely unpredictable. His cries and angry vocalizations change in meaning on a regular basis. He can suddenly fly into an epic rage in which he throws everything in sight and spits up his mush food *Exorcist*-style. He likes to pee in your face whenever possible. He likes to wake you up and, just when you lie back down, wake you up again. He has grown temporary black hair, then fearsome yellow scales, then new blond hair on his head, which has finally regained a normal shape. He might demand solid foods with the voracious appetite of a whole-cow-swallowing python, or refuse them with the casual indifference of a chipmunk with a cheek stash.

Well, there's another ongoing phase you'll deal with in the first year: teething. This phenomenon makes ordinary "growing pains" seem like a fun-filled day at the Build-A-Bear workshop. Just think about the word *teething*: there aren't too many body parts that grow so agonizingly, they get a gerund named after them.

TEETHING 101

The process of teething generally starts at around six to seven months, although some wild infants don't start to sprout teeth until twelve to eighteen months. But even before the tooth pushes through the gums (or "erupts," as dentists charmingly put it), the gums start to swell. This can be extremely irritating and painful to your untamed infant for days.

How to Help

You can help him to feel better by providing things to "chew" on, such as teething toys, a cold washcloth, or a frozen bagel (take it away before it fully thaws, as it can pose a choking hazard). Your child might bring this up in therapy years later as the "cruel bagel tease," so maybe you should stick with nonedibles. You can offer a baby bottle of ice water to suck, although some babies experience more pain with sucking.

Some parents might choose to try a local numbing agent, such as Baby Anbesol or Orajel. Opinions tend to differ on this. They tend to be difficult to apply, only work temporarily, and taste really awful. But when you're desperate, you're desperate. Talk to your wild infant's doctor before using these.

Other Possible Side Effects of Teething

Some human parents are of the opinion that teething can cause fever, diarrhea, or runny nose. Most experts beg to differ. However, if you want to be sure, take your infant's temperature. If it is higher than 101°F (or 100.4°F for a baby under three months of age), call the pediatrician.

TOOTH CARE 101

Believe it or not, you'll need to begin the ritual of grooming your untamed infant's teeth before said teeth actually arrive. This gets your little creature used to the idea of having her gums cleaned well ahead of time. Plus, it's likely she will bite you the first few times you try messing with her mouth, so why not get those bites out of the way before the sharp pointies come in?

Here are some starter tips for beginning dental hygiene for wild infants:

🐾 **Gauze Square—You don't really need an actual toothbrush prior to the existence of teeth. To start, use a gauze square (you can find these in the first-aid section** of a pharmacy). Wet it with plain water and wipe it over the baby's gums. It can pick up quite a bit of ick from your infant's mouth.

* Fingertip Brush—This is a brush with rubber bristles that sits like a cap over your finger. Or if you want, you can opt for an infant toothbrush; these are very soft. They tend to get chewed up very quickly, though.

* Positioning—Hold your young against you when brushing, facing into a mirror so you can see what you are doing. The infant, likewise, will enjoy gazing into the mirror. The untamed wild infant is less likely to snap her mouth shut or wriggle away when you come at her from this position.

* Skip the Toothpaste—Guess what you don't need at this point? If you guessed toothpaste, you really are thinking counterintuitively, aren't you? But you're also right. As much as toothpaste is associated with brushing teeth, it's not so good for wild infants. They tend to swallow it, and swallowing excess fluoride can damage the enamel of the teeth that haven't grown in yet. And although every fiber of your being might resist the idea of your infant's teeth developing sharp, hard biting capability, you don't want her to miss out on the standard tooth material. You want her to be able to eat Laffy Taffy, don't you?

ABOUT FLUORIDE

This is going to sound like a total contradiction, but wild infants over six months of age do need to have *some* fluoride in their daily diets to prevent future cavities. If your tap water is not fluoridated, you can buy bottled water that is.

- ❧ **Monkey See, Monkey Brush**—The untamed infant especially enjoys imitation, which also happens to be the highest form of flattery. So you will make things fun for the infant plus be flattered if you brush your teeth in front of her before brushing hers.
- ❧ **Name the Teeth**—Another fun approach is to name your wild infant's teeth and sing to them while you brush. You'll look deranged, but she will be amused. Plus, it will be helpful to be on a first-name basis with those teeth when they sink into your flesh, so that you can scream "No, Xavier! Stop, Penelope!"

Good luck with all that.

Chapter 11

ILLNESS IN THE WILD

Your wild infant is still such a mystery, with her erupting teeth and scaly head and multicolored poop. There is a certain odd logic to how the human body starts out, with the little soft spot on the head that will close up, the teeth that will fall out and be replaced by other teeth, the hair that will be shed and replaced by other hair. She's like a miraculous little tree, almost.

However, there are flaws to the design, and over the first few years of your wild child's life, you will probably get to know her pediatrician pretty well. Kids always seem to be getting colds, viruses, and ear infections. The immune system of the wild infant is not yet fully formed (and their ears, quite frankly, suck).

Is It a Fever?

When a wild infant is between zero and three months of age, a fever can be sign of a serious infection. Remember that the immune system of the untamed infant takes a while to develop, so an infection in the first few months of life should be taken care of right away. If your untamed infant has a fever of 100.4°F or higher, you should call the doctor. Untamed babies with fevers might have to be hospitalized and treated with antibiotics until they are better.

When you call the doctor's office, have the following information ready:

- **The pediatrician's name**
- **Your wild infant's current temperature (see next section)**
- **Your untamed baby's symptoms, starting with the ones you are most worried about, and roughly how long the symptoms have existed**
- **Information about what you've done so far for the symptoms**
- **The phone number of a pharmacy that you use (it should be one that is open, convenient, and takes your health insurance)**
- **Your wild infant's weight at her last checkup, in case the doctor wants to check on the dosage of a medication**

Taking the Temperature of the Wild Infant

If your untamed infant is under three years of age, the American Academy of Pediatrics recommends that you take his temperature rectally. This method provides the most accurate reading, and accuracy is very important, especially at this very young age.

Okay, let's get this out of the way: This is probably not going to be a great experience for your wild infant. Who would like a piece of glass or plastic stuck up their butt? But if you're quick and efficient, you can get the whole thing out of the way and have the information you need.

Before You Start

If you are using a nonmercury glass thermometer, make sure you have one intended for rectal use. If you're using a digital thermometer from your household, you should designate this the Official Rectal Thermometer by marking it *R*. Make sure all members of your family know this before they pop it in their mouths. Ew.

Clean the thermometer by wiping it with rubbing alcohol or washing it with soapy water. Then make sure it is reset by shaking it until the temperature goes down below 98.6°F. To reset a digital thermometer, just turn it off and then on again.

Do the Deed

1. Put a dab of petroleum jelly on the tip of your thermometer. Lay your untamed infant belly-down on the changing table or your lap and hold him gently but firmly, with one hand on his back. Tell him he can talk about this all he wants in therapy, but you need to know his temperature now.

2. Put another dab of petroleum jelly at the opening of his anus. Gently insert the thermometer tip a half-inch into his rectum (don't force it) and hold it between your second and third fingers, with your hand cupped over your wild baby's buttocks. If you are using a glass thermometer, wait two minutes, or if it's a digital, just wait for the sound of the beep. But don't leave a message—you won't get a call back.

A rectal temperature of 100.4°F or higher in a baby under three months is considered a fever.

MANAGING A FEVER

If your wild infant does have a fever, make sure the room of your domicile is not too warm, and the infant is not dressed too heavily. You can remove all clothes but a T-shirt, but also keep a blanket handy for when the fever drops and she gets cold.

Here are some other instructions for reducing a wild fever in your wild baby:

- ❀ Acetaminophen or Ibuprofen—After checking with your doctor and confirming the proper dose, you can give the *Kingdomius infantius* specimen a fever-reducing medicine, such as acetaminophen or ibuprofen (never aspirin). After giving this medicine, you should start to see the fever come down thirty minutes later, sometimes sooner.
- ❀ Bathtime—Another way to bring a baby's fever down is to give her a bath in a few inches of lukewarm water, using a washcloth to spread water over her.
- ❀ Hydrate—Make sure your feverish untamed infant has much to drink, since she is sweating out a lot of fluids. Dehydration tends to only make a fever feel worse.

THE YUCKY STUFF

In addition to the regular healthy nastiness that your wild infant will secrete, excrete, and expel from his mouth and other orifices, there are also unhealthy types of grossitude that you will want to look out for.

This is kind of confusing, since your infant is doing all sorts of gross things regularly, and those are mostly okay. In fact, most of what he does is downright disgusting, but in most cases, it's also worthy of applause. However, there are types of poop and vomit that are not so super. It's your exciting job to discern the fine line between "gross" and "sick." It's like the difference between a gigantic, steaming pile of elephant dung (gross poop), and a steaming pile of elephant dung that is used to paint a portrait of the Virgin Mary (totally *sick* poop). That painting really exists, by the way.

For so-called "sick poop" and vomit, you will want to call the doctor, ASAP.

JUNGLE PLAYDATE

Look, if you have to mate with a guy who's a tree-dwelling primate, the marmoset is the way to go. Mr. Marmoset gives piggyback rides to the kids, *and* he grooms and feeds them, while Ma Marmoset pretty much sits back and gets a mani-pedi. What a guy! Experts say the reason Mr. Marmoset is so sweet is because childbirth puts a tremendous strain on the mom. Apparently, giving birth to marmoset babies is equivalent to a 120-pound woman squeezing out a 30-pound kid. WTF? No wonder she's tired! Okay, but settle down, Alanis Marmoset—sure, you suffered, but with a lot of help! Mr. Marmoset also acts as a midwife during delivery! He actually eats the afterbirth for his lady. When's the last time you saw a man eat afterbirth who wasn't a contestant on *Fear Factor*? Mr. Marmoset: Father of the Year!

- -

Diarrhea

Diarrhea in newborn wild infants can cause dehydration rather quickly. The question is, with all of the tarry poop, black poop, pasty poop, and Dijon mustard poop, how do you know when it's diarrhea and when it's not? One rule of thumb is that if it looks more like water than like mustard, it might be diarrhea. Also, if your untamed baby is pooping out more than he is eating, this could be a sign of diarrhea. Call your doctor with questions. The pediatrician might just be the one person in the world who won't mind hearing a detailed description of your baby's poop.

Vomiting

Sure, you might have grown accustomed to the garden-variety breastmilk or formula spitup that your wild infant so enjoys, but there's also bad vomit. The bad kind is projectile vomit, which shoots out of the mouth as opposed to dribbling down the chin. If your infant is doing this, it might mean that he has an obstruction in the valve between the stomach and the small intestine. You should call your doctor about this right away.

Also, if your untamed baby vomits after more than three feedings in a row, this might cause dehydration. Definitely also call the doctor if blood appears in the vomit, if vomiting continues for more than twenty-four hours, or if your baby seems listless and "not quite right."

Dehydration

If your infant hasn't peed in eight hours, you should call the doctor. Not peeing could mean your untamed baby is dehydrated.

Floppiness

Yes, I know "floppy" is a good way of describing most wild infants in general. However, he also squirms a lot and manically waves his arms and legs around, doesn't he? If your untamed baby seems totally floppy and without muscle tone, have the doctor take a look.

The Shakes

If your untamed infant seems to be quivering all over, call your doctor.

Signs of Illness in An Older Infant

Once your wild offspring has passed the one-month mark, you don't necessarily need to keep calling your pediatrician like you're trying to win a call-in radio contest. However, some signs of sickness that do merit a phone call include the following:

- **Ongoing Fever**—Has a fever lasting more than two days.
- **Stiff Neck**—Has a fever and a stiff neck (test for a stiff neck by holding a favorite toy at face level and then moving it toward the ground. If she can't follow the toy by bringing her chin down to her chest, or if she seems to be in pain while doing so, she might have a stiff neck). A stiff neck along with a fever might be a sign of meningitis.
- **Seems Unusually Sleepy**—That's right, if your baby suddenly starts sleeping a lot, you still don't get to break out the champagne. A sudden increase in sleep is not normal and might indicate an infection.
- **Cries Excessively**—This is beyond the excessive crying that is more or less normal. You might be too tired to know what normal even means anymore, so just call the doctor.
- **Vomits Persistently**—After every feeding within a twelve-hour period, or has vomit containing blood.
- **Seems Dehydrated**—Is peeing a lot less than usual.
- **Has Trouble Breathing**—You might notice the skin between her ribs sucks in with each breath. Also call the doctor if she is breathing too rapidly (more than forty breaths per minute).
- **Has Ongoing Blue-ish Lips or Fingernails**—Ah, the rainbow of colors that is your baby! Sometimes babies turn blue from the cold or from crying. But if it is continuous, this is a matter for the doctor.

- ❖ Has a Cough—Particularly a whooping or barking cough. Not to be confused with all the other bizarre sounds your wild infant makes.
- ❖ Has Eye Inflammation or Discharge (not only from vigorous crying).
- ❖ Has a Rash—Specifically one covering most of her body.

SICKNESS SUPPLIES

Yes, we have once again arrived at the portion of our program called "supply time."

You will need a whole bunch of stuff for taking care of all sorts of wild infant health anomalies. Exactly what you'll need will depend on what sort of illnesses your wild infant runs into, so it's impossible to list everything. Here's a list of some of the most common:

- ❖ Thermometers, at least one oral and one rectal (ouch!)
- ❖ Infant acetaminophen drops or suspension
- ❖ Infant ibuprofen drops
- ❖ Vaseline
- ❖ Pedialyte—Oral electrolyte solution designed to replace fluids and minerals lost from diarrhea or vomiting (not an extreme sports drink for wild infants after mountain climbing or bungee jumping)
- ❖ Benadryl—Antihistamine for allergic reactions
- ❖ Calibrated syringes or droppers for giving medicines
- ❖ Nasal aspirator—It's about as fun as it sounds
- ❖ Saline nose drops—They help break up stuffy noses
- ❖ Diaper rash cream
- ❖ Hydrocortisone cream
- ❖ Oatmeal bath for skin problems

ADMINISTERING MEDICINES

Whew. Your little one had a fever, and the pediatrician told you what medicine to give your primitive little creature, and instructed you on how much to give. However, remember we are talking about a wild, totally untamed little being, and there's a very good chance he is not going to take his medicine like a champ. In fact, it's more likely than not that the dropperful of Tylenol you just squirted into his mouth is going to be regurgitated right back out, either in a dribble on his chin or in a defiant spray into your face. Then you might try desperately to cram it back in with your fingers, to absolutely no avail. Why can't you just switch your breast secretion setting from "milk" to "Tylenol" on command? Well, because that would just be too easy, and then everyone in the world would be after your breasts.

SKIP THE ASPIRIN

The American Academy of Pediatrics does not recommend that children take aspirin of any kind, even the kind labeled "Children's Aspirin." Aspirin is linked to a neurological disease called Reye's syndrome.

Instead, try these fun scenarios for trying to get medicine down your unhappy little infant's gullet.

Two-Person Maneuver

This little trick takes two adult humans to be effective. One adult sits on the floor, leaning against a wall, legs straight out in front of him. The other lays the baby on Adult One's legs, so the infant's head is slightly higher than his body and the baby's feet point toward Adult One's feet. Adult One then moves the baby's arms away from his head, which keeps him from knocking the medicine away.

Adult Two slips the medicine dropper into the side of the baby's mouth, between his cheeks and the future molars that will bite the shit out of you once they arrive. Adult Two, a brave soul, then squirts in a few drops of the medicine, then a few more, and then a few more until the dropper is empty. The beauty of this is that it doesn't matter if the baby's mouth is shut or if it is wide open in a rictus of screeching misery; the medicine will dribble down his throat regardless.

Cheek Pocket

Another method that is a little less elaborate and can feasibly be done by one human is the cheek pocket. Use a finger to pull out a corner of your baby's mouth, making a "pocket" in his cheek, and drop the medicine into the pocket a little at a time. Keep the pocket open until all the medicine has been swallowed. Do not try to use the cheek pocket for storing loose change, credit cards, or photos of your infant. You will never see them again.

Use the Art of Distraction

Almost all wild infants tolerate unpleasantries much better if there is a veritable circus sideshow of distractions going on in front of them. Have another adult or wild sibling wave a toy, voice a puppet, make funny faces, or ride a unicycle in front of your wild infant as she is being given the medicine. If you are the only human around, you can dangle a toy from your mouth as you use both hands to dispense the medication. **Note**: If it's just you, do *not* ride a unicycle during this operation. It will make things super complicated.

Don't Hide It

Trying to "hide" medicine in food or a milk bottle is not recommended. It will probably taste like ick coated with yuck with a shot of barf. Plus, if your infant stops drinking it, which she will, you will have no idea how much of the dosage she actually drank.

CONSIDER SUPPOSITORIES

If your wild and crazy infant puts up a continuous struggle against receiving her medicine orally, talk to your pediatrician about acetaminophen suppositories (oh, snap!). The dosage in milligrams is the same as for oral meds, but is less desirable because the amount absorbed can vary. It's also less desirable because it goes up the baby's butt. See if this might not convince the wild one to make a cheek pocket!

INFECTIOUS RASHES

In addition to the regular old diaper rash your untamed infant might acquire from his wild and crazy diaper situation, there are also a few rashes that go along with infectious diseases. They're as fun to look at as they are to describe.

One good thing: you probably won't have to worry about some of the more notorious rashes like measles, rubella, or chickenpox, since your antibodies will protect your untamed offspring more or less until he is vaccinated.

Interestingly, the rashes that are most common to specimens of *Kingdomius infantius* sound a lot like Dr. Seuss titles. They are Coxsackie, roseola, and fifth disease. Here's the lowdown.

Coxsackie

This rash is also known as hand, foot, and mouth disease. Why is that, you ask? Ding-ding-ding! You are correct; it's because this rash is found on the hands, feet, and inside the mouth. It is also found on the butt, but I guess they couldn't call it "hand, foot, mouth, and butt disease" and still be taken seriously.

The rash appears as spots, and the mouth spots often blister, making swallowing uncomfortable. It's very likely that your untamed infant will be very unhappy with this condition. It usually comes with a fever, but has few long-term complications. Keep nursing a younger baby, and give an older baby a frozen juice pop to soothe the throat. You can also try giving an older baby half a teaspoon of a liquid antacid to coat the ulcers.

Coxsackie can last for as long as a week, and is very contagious. Have a nice week!

Roseola

By the time you see a rash from roseola, this bad boy will be almost done plaguing your little wild child. The symptom that is way more alarming is the fever that goes with it. Fevers associated with roseola can go as high as 105°F. The fever typically lasts three to four days, and is rarely accompanied by any other symptoms. Then the fever will go away, and pink-red dots will show up on your infant's trunk, neck, and arms. Roseola is contagious until the spots disappear.

The overall incubation period is twelve days. You probably already called your doctor when your infant registered that high of a fever, and the pediatrician probably told you what to do. Once those little bumps appear, you are almost in the clear. See, it even rhymes!

Fifth Disease

Fifth disease is also known as "slapped cheek disease" because your baby's face will be bright red, as if her cheeks were slapped. If you did slap your baby's cheeks, what kind of monster are you? I'm calling the authorities.

This rash also travels to the arms and legs, then to other parts of the body. It tends to last for a few days but might go on for weeks, reappearing when the weather gets warmer than usual. This is a fairly harmless virus and only leads to complications in pregnant women. Which, presumably, is not a category that applies to you or your partner at the moment. Fifth disease is contagious for a week before the rash appears.

Chapter 12

PLAYTIME

For a while, in the beginning, your wild infant's job description was something like this:

Must be proficient at pooping, peeing, devouring human milk or formula, and screaming. Erratic sleep habits preferred. Must enjoy a fast-paced environment of waking parents while crying and kicking legs furiously. Apply within the womb.

Then, after a while of that, your untamed baby took on the more challenging tasks of eating mush food, toying with finger food, and erupting those horrible teeth out of his gums.

At some point in time, your industrious little infant acquired a new job responsibility: Play. The updated ad might read:

Must enjoy throwing the same toy on the floor over and over and over and over. Never-ending surprise at the big eye reveal in peekaboo strongly preferred. Must love messes.

Why Play?

The need to play is not unique to *Kingdomius infantius* specimens—many types of animal engage in behaviors that seem to have no real purpose but shits and giggles. Look at those adorable panda cubs going down slides, or otters chasing after butterflies. And don't even get me started on kittens. These animals take "silly" to a whole new level, and at the same time, they're developing skills they'll need in adulthood. Alertness, speed, dexterity—all of these traits serve an animal in the wild, when it might mean the difference between eating dinner and being dinner.

For human young, it's not quite so dramatic, but play is still an important task. Here are some reasons why play is such an important part of your wild baby's job during the first year of life:

- ❀ **Socialization—Play is a necessary developmental milestone. Playing with other humans gives your wild infant a valuable opportunity to connect.**
- ❀ **Power—Playing with inanimate objects allows wild infants to assert their power and have an impact on their environment. This might be a destructive impact, depending on the object, but it's educational nonetheless.**
- ❀ **Solitude—Playing independently gives the wild infant the chance to connect with himself, and gives you a minute to reconnect with your favorite TV show (while never taking your eyes off the wild infant, of course).**

Look for "Toys" You Already Have

Before you head out to purchase everything in Toys "R" Us, try using some common household items to amuse your young for hours on end. Here are a few of these.

Containers

The wild infant is naturally drawn to containers of every kind. Plastic food storage containers are a big hit with most untamed infants. She will enjoy these containers empty, but will also love them with something to dump out of them, such as water, sand, oatmeal (dry, of course), and birdseed. The wild infant very much enjoys the act of upending things and dumping them on the ground. The more horrified you are at this act, the more the wild infant tends to enjoy it.

Remote Control

The untamed infant is quite savvy to the ways of the adults in her tribe, and has most likely taken note that the TV remote control is a highly prized possession, often fought over. Therefore, she, too, will want this coveted item, and might try to lunge toward you and grab it right out of your hands (she is so sick of watching professional golf!).

And don't think you can fool her with one of those cheesy "toy" remotes either, with the big bright colors and the buttons that play silly songs. She's smarter than that. Your best bet is to find an old remote control, remove the batteries, tape the battery cover back on, and let her go to town. She will be totally happy until she realizes *Dora the Explorer* isn't coming on.

Kitchen Cabinet Raid

Basically, your precocious little wild infant will want to make your toys her toys. Therefore, she will want to get into your kitchen cabinets and raid your cooking equipment. (Just wait until she's an adult and actually cooks and cleans for real—she sure won't want that stuff anymore!) Although most of your cabinets will probably be babyproofed, fill a few designated drawers or cabinets with stuff she can safely empty out.

BUYING TOYS—STICK WITH THE CLASSICS

After a while, you may need to branch out and get your wild infant some actual toys to play with. And even if you manage to avoid Toys "R" Us for as long as humanly possible, others will start asking you what to buy your baby for his first birthday. Good question! You can't very well instruct friends to gift your child with a nonfunctioning remote control, can you?

Ever wonder why the same baby toys tend to stick around for generations and generations? Wow, then you're pretty slow. They stick around because infants love them! Certain types of toys just naturally engage the imagination of the wild infant. They love noise; they love imitation; and they love repetition. Anyone who has watched a wild infant press the same button two thousand times in a row can confirm this truth.

Here are a few classic toys sure to fascinate the mind of your untamed offspring:

- ☸ **Rattles—Even very young wild infants who have almost no motor skills, can barely focus their eyes, and list "sitting up" as their long-term goal can wave a rattle. You can use the rattle yourself to teach the wild offspring how to follow sounds. Rattles are excellent entertainment tools during diaper changing.**
- ☸ **Nesting Cups—In a sense, these are your untamed youth's first puzzle. They also can stack for building, pour, be sorted into colors, and be counted. They are excellent for learning and fun. Nesting dolls can also teach the wild infant about pregnancy. Ha, not really.**
- ☸ **Stacking Toys—Wild babies love plastic or wooden rings that stack up on a post. You will also want lots of blocks, for touching, tasting, and banging together. Not for eating.**
- ☸ **Button-Pushing Toys—This is an excellent lesson in cause and effect, and wild infants absolutely cannot get enough of them. You could try a toy where a button is**

pushed and a train spins around, a funny animal pops up, etc. Theoretically, a light switch could also fall into this category, but this might not be safe. And besides, do you want your lights flickering on and off all day long?

❤ **Toys That Imitate Your Activities**—From the very youngest age, wild infants love to imitate grownups. There is something about adulthood that seems so magical to them. Wait until they find out, huh? Then they'll become adults who keep acting like kids. In the meantime, wild infants adore bowls, spoons, toy phones, toy vacuum cleaners, dolls, mops, a toddler-sized stroller, or a shopping cart. It's too bad some of these cleaning appliances don't actually work!

BABY GENIUS!

Don't go rushing out to buy a bunch of educational toys that are meant to help your infant earn her doctorate degree before she's potty trained. Know that there is a natural order to the things she's supposed to be learning, and her curriculum is pretty much full right now. It's all about Intro to Teething, Potty 101, Advanced Motor Skills, Grownup Imitation (Honors Course), and Major in Tantruming.

The point is, let her learn her skills at a developmentally appropriate time. If you want to teach your infant something a bit beyond her current level, do so with patience. She might catch on and enjoy it; but if not, you can go back to it later. There really is no rush.

TOY SAFETY

There are some basic criteria your wild infant's toys should meet so he can use them safely. Here are some of them:

❤ **Nontoxic**—The paint should be nontoxic.
❤ **No Small Parts**—The toy should have no small or detachable parts (infants eat everything).

- ❦ **No Sharp Edges**—None of the edges or corners of the toy are sharp.
- ❦ **Shhh!**—None of the bells or whistles from the toys are at ridiculously high decibels (this is for your sanity as well).
- ❦ **No "Bean Bag" Stuffing**—The pellets inside these toys are a choking hazard and you have no reason to believe your wild infant will not try to eat them.
- ❦ **The String Rule**—No loose cords, strings, or ribbons longer than 12 inches, or anything that can get tangled around the wild infant's throat.
- ❦ **The Tube Rule of Thumb**—The toy should be too large to fit inside a toilet paper tube. Anything smaller is a choking hazard. Actual toilet paper tubes probably aren't great, either. I mean, can't you at least splurge on a paper towel tube?
- ❦ **Unleaded**—The toy has no lead.
- ❦ **No Phthalates**—The toy should not contain phthalates. These are sometimes used in plastic toys to make the plastic soft. Some people think they contain hazardous chemicals.
- ❦ **No Recall**—There has not been a recall issued for that version of the toy.

FUN BABY GAMES

Like most humans, wild infant humans also enjoy playing games. However, at this stage, your untamed creature probably lacks the intelligence and motor skills to play a game of chess or badminton with you. Peekaboo and "ankle ride" are a lot closer to his speed. These games might seem pointless and completely inane to you (how do you even win a game of peekaboo?), but to an infant human, they are endlessly exciting.

The most exciting feature about baby games is repetition. If you can do the same thing over and over and over again (while pretending that it's a total surprise each time), you will be the total hit of the baby community. Wild infants will book you as the entertainment for all of their get-togethers. "OMG, have you seen her act? She puts her hands over her eyes and then uncovers them, and the eyes are totally still there! You are not going to believe this shit. She's amazing."

Besides repetition, you should choose games that engage more than one of the five senses, and teach a lesson. Here are some ideas.

"Hide and Seek"

I put this in quotes, because there is really no actual hiding or seeking involved. Start this game with an infant of at least a month old. Lay him down in the middle of the room and move around the room, talking to him. As he scours the room for the source of the sound of your voice, he will start to associate sights and sounds. No, you don't even need to have him cover his eyes and count. He's that clueless, that even when he watches you walk away, you can "hide" from him. Plus, he doesn't know how to count anyway. This game gets way more exciting once your wild infant is actually able to crawl, and understands approximately who you are.

The game also teaches "object permanence"—in other words, when mom is gone, she will come back. (P.S. Make sure you do come back, or this game will just be a terrible trauma.)

Ah, Boo

Place your wild infant, facing you, on your lap. Look him in the eyes. Say "Ahhh," then lean forward, gently bump foreheads, and say "Boo!" This teaches your untamed infant to anticipate you—eventually, he will start to lean forward to meet you. Unless you bang heads too hard, in which case he will begin to cry when you initiate this game. (**Note**: You can probably alternate other words or nonsense fragments for "Ah, Boo," since your wild infant doesn't understand these words anyway. You can try, "Blah . . . BLAH!" or "Yada . . . Yada!" or "Learn . . . English!" The kid won't be offended in the least.

Ankle or Knee Rides

There's nothing quite like a rousing game of "ankle/knee ride." Sit down and put the wild infant on your knees, facing you, or straddling your ankles, lying forward against your legs. Support him firmly under the arms as you bounce him gently (don't jounce the infant off your leg!) to the rhythm of some beloved rhyme. This teaches rhythm, balance, and anticipation as he hears the rhyme repeated over and over.

You can also play the "inverted knee ride" by lying down on a rug, and bringing your knees up above your chest. Hold your calves parallel to the floor, and place your baby stomach-down on your calves, head peeking over your knees. Bounce him gently with your legs, or rock him from side to side. Make sure you don't get too vigorous about this exercise, since sending your infant hurtling into the air is not a great way to get your kid interested in games. Plus, it will probably deter him from ever wanting to become an astronaut.

Peekaboo

And here is the classic wild infant game. Cover your face with a baby blanket or burp cloth (or just your hands if you'd rather not stick your face directly into stale burps). Then whisk either the cloth or your hands away dramatically, saying, "Peekaboo!" or whatever nonsense phrase suits your fancy. No profanity, please.

This game also teaches object permanence, which means that when something goes away, it doesn't go away forever. This will be a nice lesson, at least until your infant begins playing gambling games where his money does go away forever.

Play Station(s)

Once you've played peekaboo for two hours straight, you might decide it's a perfect time to encourage your little one to enjoy some alone time. Or, to put it much more scientifically, "independent play." Learning how to entertain himself is a valuable skill for wild infants *and* wild adult humans, but you can't just abandon the little guy. Here are some tips for making solo play fun:

- 🐾 **Move Around**—Set up a series of "play stations" in your habitat, and move your wild infant from one to the next, letting him explore something new at each station.
- 🐾 **Nice View**—If he's not moving around yet, you can position an infant swing so the wild child can look outside.
- 🐾 **On the Floor**—Put a quilt on the floor and scatter a few toys on it, within the wild infant's reach.

Taking your infant from station to station will keep him entertained for up to one glorious hour!

SOCIAL MILESTONES

Your wild infant is hitting physical milestones every day—she's cutting teeth, eating finger foods, pooping solid matter, sleeping at night, making valiant attempts to sleep *through* the night, and sitting up.

But in addition to these amazing physical strides in her development, she's also developing her little brain and her feelings. She's figuring out what she likes (throwing things on the ground) and what she *really* likes (you picking the things up again), what she doesn't like (the rectal thermometer), and she's starting to suspect that when you cover your eyes, you're going to uncover them theatrically and say some gibberish at her. These are milestones of a different, but no less important, variety.

Have a Playdate

Believe it or not, your wild infant will also begin to need social interaction with infants her own age. Even if all the two infants do is lie on a blanket, drool while staring at each other, and poop their pants, you should still make time to get them together. Really, are adult dates all that much better?

Speaking of . . . you, too, probably need some human company. Adult humans who have recently spawned wild infants can relate to each other in a way few other beings can. You can discuss your approaches to getting sleep at night, or trade stories about the "cheek pocket" medicine method. Or you can just lie on a blanket and drool all afternoon, too. It's your party!

Researchers originally thought wild infants barely acknowledged each other's presence when placed in the same room with each other. They believed that the infants would simply imitate each other while pretending they totally didn't even see each other over there. Now, scientists have uncovered that this is a total crock of shit. Apparently, they look at each other with blatant interest. And by six months, they begin to develop rudimentary games, such as "call and response." Here's how this game is played.

Wild Infant One: Waaaaaaaaaah!

Wild Infant Two: Waaaaaaaaah!

That's about all there is to that game.

The peer relationships between two wild infants are different from those with adult human parents or siblings. These interactions will evolve over time based on the level of development and skills of the babies involved. For example, two wild infants on a blanket who are two months old will probably just look at one another. At three months of age, they may try to touch each other. At seven or eight months, the infants might attempt to crawl over to one another, or to hand each other a toy.

At fifteen years old, the babies on the blanket will simply text one another.

Playgroups

So, where are you supposed to find these other infants to socialize with your untamed infant? You've pretty much been holed up in your home, devoid of sleep and with dried formula all stuck in your hair and on your clothes. You've been talking back to Elmo, and you think he's been answering you. In other words, your social skills are not exactly at their best right now either. So what do you do? Do you just go out, grab the nearest baby, and tell the mom to follow you if she ever wants to see her infant again? This is not a good start. No, no. Do not do this.

One approach is to join or start a playgroup. Look into whether there is a mothers' club in your area. Most mothers' clubs sponsor playgroups. Or you can attend a parenting class at your local hospital—this is a good way to meet potential parent friends or playgroup organizers. Or spend time out walking with your wild infant, and get the phone numbers of other wild-infant-walking parents. Try to get at least five or six other parents, and try to get your group to meet at least weekly.

Just Playin'

Many species of animals play with their young, and according to *Scientific American*, researchers still aren't sure exactly why. Decades of studies as to why animals play have left these scientists shrugging and saying, "I guess it's just fun." Studies of "play hunting" haven't conclusively found that these games have led to better hunting skills in adult animals. One recent theory is that rough play among animals might help babies become used to experiencing a stress response. Once they have this mastered, they won't be as freaked out in adulthood, when some seriously stressful shit goes down (like a lion attack).

Emotional Milestones

Don't worry—your wild infant isn't exactly ready to go out on his first date yet. But you will begin to notice some pretty impressive behaviors emerging in your young, ones that are both cute and very much human. You will begin to see past the mysteriously squirmy, scaly-headed mole rat that first came out of you or your partner's body, and get a glimpse of the little person your baby will soon be. It's at moments like these that the job of being an adult human parent begins to be fun. When you can ask people, "Guess what my baby did today?" and the answer isn't, "Spit puréed chicken all over my face," you know things are getting good.

Enjoy these milestones when they happen, but remember, don't push the poor infant to get there before he's ready. You don't want to be a weird stage mom, do you? Just FYI, *nobody* likes that lady.

Early Stuff

These behaviors might not exactly knock your socks off, but they're a start. As a newborn, your untamed infant will be able to recognize the voices of you and your partner, as well as the voices of people who surrounded his mother during pregnancy (so yes, if you or your female partner worked while pregnant, your wild infant might just know your boss's voice. Ick). He will also know the voices of siblings, or even the cast members of the mom's favorite TV show (so please, ma, no *Jersey Shore*. Have mercy on your wild infant, if not yourself!). The infant will notice if the maternal parent is feeling stressed out, and will become anxious by extension. Ugh, it is so stressful being a wild infant!

Smiles

By four to eight weeks of age, the untamed infant will begin to display smiling behavior that is unrelated to a gas bubble. At around two months of age, the infant will likely turn his head in the direction of a parent's voice and gaze directly into your eyes like it's a staring contest.

LOL

At about four months, the untamed infant will exhibit his first laugh, and will continue to do so whenever you naively think you're going to get some sleep. Nothing makes a baby laugh more than an adult human's plans. Your infant will also begin to squeal, wriggle, and breathe heavily from excitement or happiness at this point.

Anger

Uh-oh. You thought your untamed infant was plenty wild enough with the late-night shrieking, the explosive pooping, and the spitting up of various foods and liquids onto your face or body. But no, at around six months, it really starts to get good. At this stage, your untamed infant begins to develop genuine, deep-seated anger and white-hot rage, like a wolverine that just ate a porcupine. This will be different from the sounds of exhaustion or irritation, which have already made themselves known through ear-splitting cries. This will be flat-out indignation at the injustice of a favorite toy rolling out of his reach. Who do you think you are, Lovey? How dare you?

Anger is still a good milestone, though, because this rage is supposedly "motivating." In other words, if your infant's lovey has rolled out of reach, the angry little creature might just have enough incentive to crawl over to the lovey and grab it. Good job, baby!

Your infant will also begin to recognize anger in your voice, too, so be careful about the tone you take with a wild infant once they reach this point.

Stranger Anxiety

Around the six-month mark, another iffy emotional "skill" will show up: stranger anxiety. Before this time, your untamed infant will be a squirmy, clueless little blob who you can hand off to just about any old person without him knowing or caring. Not anymore. Now, when you try to let a stranger care for your infant, it's not going to fly—there will be screams; there will be cries; there will possibly be little fists connecting with big faces. Oops!

Stranger anxiety will be a bit of a pain because you won't be able to just pass off your kid to that homeless guy outside the store while you get some shopping done. Ha! That was a joke, and also a test. If you thought that scenario was okay, I've clearly failed you in my instruction. You need to go back and read this book again.

But seriously: stranger anxiety will make it tough to leave your infant with the sitter, or take him into daycare, or endure your once-a-year visit with your in-laws (but of course, you're a little scared of them, too!).

To some extent, you might just have to wait for this phase to pass, while letting others know about the issue. Maybe instruct strangers to give him a little space at first, perhaps sit across the room and ignore him for a while until he approaches them. Most sitters or daycare providers will already know about stranger anxiety, and will know how to handle it.

STRANGER DANGER!

If your infant has stranger anxiety, make sure you're not reinforcing the fear. When someone at the mall says, "What a beautiful baby!" do you clutch him defensively and say, "Stay away from my child, you psycho!"? When you bring your baby to daycare, do you sob profusely? This is not going to help your infant. In fact, it might cause him to grow up into a cabin-inhabiting manifesto writer.

Separation Anxiety

Yet another anxiety will be coming to a household near you at about eight months. This one is all about the primary caregiver, or the person the wild infant interacts with the most. The wild infant is a very savvy creature, and understands intuitively that the being that provides him with food, clean clothes, and superfun games is pretty much the awesomest person alive. Therefore, the infant will become incredibly attached to this source of just about everything, and will become crestfallen when this individual is out of sight for even a minute. This behavior is not unique to the human species; many animals become overly attached to a caregiver just as they're about to move independently. This is why baby birds have to be kicked out of the nest. Talk about tough love! But I guess that's why you don't meet too many birds who grow up to be "mama's boys."

For your baby, it's a little less harsh. Humans have it a lot easier than other species. You're not going to ask him to pack his bags, but that's what his fear is all about. So if he's acting clingy, just pick him up and cuddle him. Applaud his attempts at exploring; nod your approval when he moves across the room, but move slowly so he can catch up with you. As he gains independence and realizes you're not going to abandon him, he will start to become more confident and less anxious.

You can also hand him his lovey during times you need to be apart. Poor old lovey; playing second fiddle again!

Chapter 13

LEAVING THE JUNGLE

So, now you have welcomed a wild infant into your habitat, and she has adjusted to her new ecosystem, more or less. She is comfortable in her crib; she is all about her favorite blanket and her lovey; she enjoys playing at her various play stations, and opening up your cabinets for extra toys. She's graduated to the grownup bathtub with all of her favorite toys. Your home is completely babyproofed, and your family dog happily cleans up baby spills. You've created a special jungle just for her, and she roams it like she is the queen of that jungle. As we've said, just when you start feeling complacent, life will throw you a curve. That's right, you'll have to leave your fragile ecosystem— whether briefly or for a (gasp) overnight stay.

SERIOUSLY, LEAVE YOUR HOUSE

So, once you have your feral creature adjusted to this new ecosystem, how do you venture out of your domicile and into the uncharted wilderness?

It's actually not that difficult. Wild infants are very portable, actually much more so than wild toddlers, for example. They really don't know where they're going most of the time, but they find new sights, smells, and sounds to be interesting.

In fact, you should really try to take your wild infant out of her habitat every day. It will be interesting for her, and it will stop the wild adult female from becoming an insane jungle loon in your home ecosystem. Fresh air never hurt any human.

Supplying Yourself for Exploration

You knew this was coming. More gear!

Maybe it's time for a major migration, such as that dreaded out-of-town in-law visit, or maybe you simply need to forage for food and emergency "baby weight" clothes at the nearest shopping center. (**Note**: Dads usually do not require "baby weight" clothes, but you never know; there may have been sympathetic weight gain during pregnancy.) Depending on whether you're transporting your young for the day or for a lengthy trip, you'll need some or all of the following supplies:

- 🐾 **Car Seat: Car seats are essential for safe migration with your offspring. Clearly, you already have one because you managed to get the infant home from the hospital, and have probably already visited the pediatrician 212 times.**

- 🐾 **Stroller: As untamed as your infant thinks she is, her wild antics are somewhat limited by her inability to walk or sit upright. Which is great, actually, because her decision-making skills are also terrible. When transporting your wild baby while she's an infant, you should have a stroller that fully reclines so she can snooze. You can also use a Snap-N-Go, which is a metal frame that converts your infant car seat into a stroller. These are useful until your baby can sit up; then she'll probably want to be in more of a traditional stroller setup. Look out, world!**

- 🐾 **Jogging or Off-Road Stroller: If your excessive food foraging has left you with some unwanted weight, you may need to take a swift, mini-migration on foot. Your young can accompany you in a jogging stroller. These strollers are also easier to maneuver on and off of sidewalks. And who knows? Maybe your baby's first words will be, "Pick up the pace, loser!" Aww.**

- **Rain Cover for Stroller:** Your untamed infant is quite vulnerable to the elements. Being torrentially rained on is very likely to cause discomfort and fussiness the likes of which you must pray to never see. If you might get caught outside in inclement weather, get one of these.

- **Sling and/or Front Carrier:** This human "pouch" is crucial to pleasant and fuss-free travel. If the idea of getting your baby—or yourself—into a sling leaves you in a state of flight-or-fight panic, try a front carrier. This is a more intuitive type of "baby-wearing" that doesn't make your infant look so much like a broken arm. Most wild babies do equally well with either pouch. More on this subject next.

- **Portable Crib or Play Yard:** Your in-laws may offer a suitable enclosure for your baby, but the last time they did this, the structure was ancient, rickety, jail-like, and easily gnawed through by your savagely teething baby. Best to bring your own. The foldable Graco Pack 'n Play is a popular option.

- **Diaper Bag:** If there is one thing you have learned quickly about your untamed infant, it is that her poop is truly a wild thing unto itself, sort of like an electrical storm (and where there's thunder, there's usually lightning). You cannot be too prepared for poop precipitation events of every shape, size, and consistency. So you'll need diapers, wipes, extra clothes, a toy to entertain her while you change her, and on and on and on it goes.

- **Portable High Chair:** As your untamed baby starts eating finger foods, she'll become a participant in meals instead of just a bystander. While this is an important developmental phase, it will leave your host's dining room looking like an abstract painting gone terribly wrong. A clip-on portable high chair will fit in the bottom of a duffel bag, and may save more relationships than any other clip-on thing ever. Well, except maybe those wavy clip-on ponytails. Those are awesome.

YOUR HUMAN POUCH: CONSTRUCTING A SLING

Like the kangaroo's joey (*Macropus rufus*), the untamed baby often enjoys being carried in a pouch against your body. Once you know how to wear a sling, your baby can hear your heartbeat, see your face, and get carried around almost as stylishly as Paris Hilton's Chihuahua.

In a sling, the baby's weight is evenly distributed on your back, so you're comfortable. And, like the kangaroo, a sling leaves both your hands free to forage for grub or start boxing another kangaroo who was totally talking about you behind your back.

Unlike putting a baby in a front pack, which has a clear place for her head, arms, and legs to go, securing a baby in a sling is not so intuitive. Your best bet is to get an experienced slingwearer to show you. (**Note**: A person who frequently injures his arm does not count.)

If you don't have a baby-wearing friend to assist you, you can review the following images for one method. (**Note**: Slings come in different sizes. Make sure yours fits your height and/or weight, as well as the weight of your baby.)

1. In your left hand, hold the sling by the ring, so the padded area (if there is one) is facing you, and the unpadded area is away from you.

2. Put the sling down on a couch, and smooth it out so that the ring is on the left end and the widest area is on the right. Open up the section that's on the bottom.

3. Place your baby on his or her back on the opened fabric so the head comes within a hand's width of the ring and the feet are pointed toward the widest end. Your baby's

The sling

Place baby in the sling

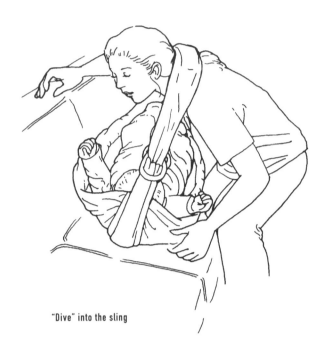

"Dive" into the sling

Final position

sudden diaper explosion should be located . . . nowhere near you.

4. Raise your right arm in the air, next to your ear, and dive into the sling with your arm and head (do not "dive" as if you will land in a swimming pool. You won't, I assure you). Adjust your position so the pad is on your left shoulder and the ring is near your left armpit.

5. Stand up, supporting your baby until you are sure he or she is secure. Physically secure, anyway. If you waited around for your wild infant to become emotionally, financially, and psychologically secure, you'd be slinging him when he's thirty-five. Or older. Make sure his face is not in any way crushed against your body or the fabric of the sling. He should be able to breathe freely the entire time. Also, his body shouldn't be too crumpled up—he should be able to stretch out relatively easily.

PACK THAT DIAPER BAG

One thing you will learn as a new parent to a wild infant is that your diaper bag is going to be very important, and very heavy. You will be lugging a lot of accessories when traveling with this untamed creature of yours, probably more than your mom did when you were moving to another house.

In fact, it might almost feel as though you're packing for a year in Europe instead of a day trip to the zoo. To the extent that you can keep it simple, try to do so. You'll want to pack in advance to avoid last-minute rushing around, which will stress you out and cause you to accidentally pack your grandmother's adult diapers instead of wild infant diapers. Could that work? Maybe, if your infant's butt were fifteen times larger.

Here are a few items you should have in a typical diaper bag:

❖ Diapers (at least four)
❖ A refillable pack of infant wipes

- Diaper rash ointment
- Plastic bags for messy diapers
- Light blanket (to cover wild infant, or use as play mat)
- Waterproof changing pad or rubberized sheet
- Cloth diaper (for burping and general messes)
- Sunscreen (for wild infants older than six months)
- Bottles and formula, unless you are nursing exclusively
- Food for older finger-foodie infant (Cheerios, etc.)
- A snack for you (don't go stealing his Cheerios!)
- Water bottle (for parental drink and cleanup, since dogs usually do not fit into diaper bags)
- Change of clothes for the wild infant
- Change of shirt for yourself
- Stain stick (there will be stains)
- Travel pack of tissues (there will be snot)
- A few toys or rattles (there will be boredom)

JUNGLE PLAYDATE

The female kangaroo is able to get pregnant within a few days of giving birth, and actually spends most of her life pregnant. But along with several other species, she is able to maintain an embryo in a state of dormancy for a while, until she gets the previous kid out the door. This phenomenon, called embryonic diapause, might also occur in response to unfavorable environmental conditions. It's like Mother Nature's own frozen embryo bank, minus the ridiculous overpricing!

Head Out!

Wild infants are more or less indifferent to the environments you choose for their first few excursions. But you should probably pick a place, so you're not simply driving around like some weirdo with formula spills all down your shirt.

Grocery stores, bookstores, or furniture stores are all places that will have items of interest to you, the adult human, as well as bright colors and various shapes for the infant to feast her eyes upon. In addition, these places are packed with other adult females, who will love to smile and coo at your infant as you navigate the aisles in a sleep-deprived haze.

SKIP CLOTHING-DENSE STORES

Shopping is generally an awesome idea, but steer clear of clothing stores with narrow aisles and densely packed racks. Your infant will end up with a whole bunch of mom jeans shoved in her face, and might end up breathing chemicals like formaldehyde, which is used to protect fabrics, or gnawing on sharp-edged tags. Plus, clothing stores don't like to have their clothes drooled on as a general rule.

Grocery Stores

Grocery shopping is the best form of wild infant shopping, for a lot of reasons. One, your wild infant car seat might be designed to clip into a shopping cart, or might be easily placed inside. Also, grocery stores sometimes give out helium balloons to kids, which will pretty much make your infant's day. Tie it to the cart—it'll be better than an Oscar-winning movie as far as entertainment goes. If your infant is at the finger food stage, let her help herself to the free samples. Again, it's best if she doesn't drool on the food.

Mall Rats

Wild infants will intuitively love the mall. There are all kinds of crazy sights, sounds, lights, people, and fountains. Talk to your untamed infant about the many sights you are seeing together. Just look around and keep moving; there's no need to make a purchase, necessarily, unless it will make you feel better as an adult human.

Day at the Museum

Museums also provide a wide array of brightly colored displays and pictures, and are likely to be populated with a lot of people. There will be much for the wild infant to see, even if she has zero aptitude for art appreciation. You should call ahead and see if baby backpacks or strollers are allowed at the museum you plan to visit (some don't permit them). If you are using a front carrier or a sling, this can go pretty much anywhere, so swaddle up! When your wild infant is ready to suckle, stand in front of a painting you really like, and switch paintings when you switch breasts. I hear that's how all the art critics do it!

KEEP BOTTLES HOT

If you will be taking a short outing and need to bottle-feed, fill a bottle with hot water before leaving, wrap it in a small towel, and tuck it into a foam can-holder. This insulation will keep the water warm for hours, so you can add premeasured powdered formula when the little mammal is ready to eat.

Tour Your Own Town

Try being a tourist in your own hometown by seeing the sights with your wild infant. There's something fun about viewing everyday places through a fresh, albeit visually undeveloped, pair of eyes. And there are also probably a few places you have never even had a chance to see before!

Bon Appétit . . . !

Until your untamed young begins picking at finger foods, you don't even need to worry about dining at a "family-friendly" restaurant (family friendly = willing to put up with epic spills, blood-curdling tantrums, utensil-throwing, etc.). Instead, you can actually go out to a real restaurant with tablecloths that can't be colored on!

The Joy of Dining with Newborns

The best time to transport your wild infant to public eateries is when he is in what is charmingly referred to as the "luggage stage." This means he can simply be carried along, placed down wherever, and will not squirm, scream, kick, vomit, or cause utter chaos in the dining establishment. (Do not actually place your luggage-stage infant on a baggage carousel. It might sound fun, but he will not enjoy it.)

Nevertheless, go early, since the restaurant will be less crazy and you will have more fun. If your infant is sleeping in his car seat, you might be able to safely tuck him under the table for a while. Don't forget that you have an infant under the table, though.

Another option is looking into the wooden high chairs at restaurants. Some of them invert to make stable stands for an infant seat. Test the stability of this seat before placing your infant upon it, or he will unleash the wrath of a thousand suns upon you.

If your untamed infant becomes ravenous and you are nursing, toss a napkin or nursing wrap over your shoulder and settle him in to feed. (Order a meal that's not too difficult to eat with just one hand. This means probably no hot coffee, even though that's the one thing you need more than anything in this godforsaken world. Sorry.)

If you are dining at Hooters, you might not have to do the napkin cover-up at all. Ask the manager!

Family Friendly!

Once your child is actually able to shovel food into his ravenous little face, you will need to go with the family-friendly option. You might ask yourself, how do I know if a restaurant is family friendly? Here are some signs:

- ❖ The restaurant has padded booths to absorb sound and wild-infant thrashing
- ❖ No one turned around and gasped when you entered with your wild infant
- ❖ There are balloons, maybe even ones shaped like dachshunds
- ❖ The "tablecloths" feature a pirate maze or a cuddly butterfly/kitten tableau, and come with crayons
- ❖ There are high chairs stacked in plain view
- ❖ There is a "claw crane" stuffed animal game visible
- ❖ There are chicken fingers on the menu
- ❖ Any music in the restaurant is drowned out by wild infant shrieks, adult reprimands, and defeated sighs

Dining Tips for the Finger-Foodie Infant

Believe it or not, you don't need to necessarily order off the menu when you bring your finger-foodie wild infant to a family-friendly restaurant. You can bring some of your own foods from home, and just try to keep your wild infant contented and engaged throughout your meal. Here are some tips for doing this:

- ❖ Bring Cheerios or other finger foods, and hand them out slowly, to keep your infant wanting more.
- ❖ Bring a few small toys in case the finger foods cease to interest the infant.

- 🐾 Place your order as quickly as possible, and ask for your check as soon as your food arrives. (Hate to make you eat and run, but wild infants do not have patience for waiting for the check.)

- 🐾 Skip coffee and dessert. The time that course adds really might be pushing it for the untamed infant. The fact that he allowed you to consume a salad and a full meal was very reasonable and generous of him. What do you want, a complete dining experience?

- 🐾 Tip your waitstaff heavily, if possible. The staff will remember you as a generous patron, not as the person whose infant exploded ketchup pouches all over the booth's walls and then smeared it in. Although that was pretty memorable.

- 🐾 If you didn't bring finger foods for the wild infant, check out the menu. Do the entrées come with veggies? Try a side order of steamed vegetables and cut them small or mash them up. If there are eggs on the menu, get an order of scrambled eggs, yolks only if your child is under one year old. If there's a salad bar, forage it for soft fruits and vegetables that can be cut into bite-sized pieces.

OPPOSABLE THUMBS UP!

Believe it or not, you can probably try to bring your wild infant to the movies. In the beginning, it doesn't even need to be a Pixar or animated movie featuring talking extinct animals! Wow.

Here are some tips for taking your wild infant to catch a flick:

- 🐾 Early Show—Go to an afternoon matinee on a weekday, when theaters are all but empty, or an evening show on a weeknight. This way, if your wild infant screams, squeals, or does any other socially unacceptable wild infant behavior, fewer people will be bothered.

- ❀ **Look for Special Showings**—Some movie theaters even encourage parents to bring wild babies to special showings, where fussing is okay.

- ❀ **Quick Exit**—Go for an aisle seat, in case you have to leave.

- ❀ **Lullabye**—The good news is, you probably won't need to leave! Because theaters are dark and soothing, your wild infant will probably fall asleep after nursing or drinking a bottle. If not, he might just sit back and stare at the colors and shapes.

- ❀ **Quiet Toys**—If he's acting squirmy, you can bring a few quiet cloth toys and/or teethers to keep him occupied and contented. No rattles or loud fire engine toys, please!

- ❀ **Quiet Movie**—Likewise, don't choose a loud movie with gunshots and explosions, because this will alarm your wild infant and possibly provoke a total meltdown. Plus, if he manages to fall asleep, how annoyed will you be if a sudden car chase wakes him up?

- ❀ **Pick a Chick Flick**—Chick flicks feature lots and lots of talking, and closeups of faces, all of which babies love. Plus, chick flicks are usually attended by adult human females, who will be much more tolerant of your infant than adult human males (adult human males, however, might be more tolerant of breastfeeding). Also, chick flicks are more predictable and boring, so your wild infant has a better chance of being lulled to sleep. Note: If your wild infant is a male, he might be annoyed that you took him to a Katherine Heigl movie when he was an infant, and sue you later.

- ❀ **As a Courtesy**—Make sure your wild infant turns off his cell phone or places it on vibrate mode before the feature presentation begins. Leaving it on is just rude, baby!

JUNGLE
PLAYDATE

Despite the stork's image as a sweet, friendly baby-carrier as depicted on shower invitations, there's a dark side to this lovable bird. Among black stork nestlings, newborns aren't willing to compete for dominance by attacking and killing each other. Normally, this would be awesome, but there's not always enough regurgitated stork food for the whole family. Because the siblings won't step up and fight each other to the death, Ma or Pa Stork is stuck with the task of killing weaker babies to manage their family size. This might make you think twice about getting your babies via stork delivery. My recommendation? Try having sex instead!

- -

TAKE A HIKE

If you are an athletic type who enjoys hiking nature trails, you might think you will have to stop doing that once you have acquired a wild infant. Nonsense! Wild infants are easily portable, and even provide you with extra weight for more resistance training. In fact, if you never were a hiker before, you might want to start now. The baby-wearing hike! It's all the rage!

Here's how to get started:

🐾 Start with short, easy trails, especially if you are not a seasoned hiker.

🐾 Stay out of constant sunlight, and don't forget your wild infant's hat.

🐾 Avoid trails with low branches, for obvious reasons.

- Use a front pack or carrier until your wild infant is too heavy for one, and then switch to a backpack.
- If you take your infant hiking with a backpack, bring a makeup mirror and carry it in your pocket. Pull it out from time to time to use as a "rearview mirror" for infant checks.
- You can just "hike" around your neighborhood, if you like. Look at your neighbors' gardens, and get to know neighborhood pets by name.
- Don't just hike on sunny days—how wussy would that make you and your infant? Try rain walks. Some infants like them, provided they don't get soaked. If your wild infant is in a front pack, sling, or backpack, an umbrella will protect both of you and your infant will enjoy the sound and smell of rain. Just not so much the feel of it drenching her.
- Try an evening walk, and bring a flashlight for extra infant entertainment. Disco night hike party!
- Parks and playgrounds are great, but save them for when your wild infant is sitting or crawling and can enjoy the swings or sandbox. For now, pick places that *you* like. This infant doesn't care either way, and you'll be following her playground demands soon enough.

ARE WE THERE YET!

The untamed infant's response to automobile travel tends to vary widely among individual infants. In other words, yours might either fall asleep like he's been shot with a rhinoceros tranquilizer, or shriek miserably for the entire duration. The only way to find out is to try it.

The main issue infants seem to have with car rides is utter boredom. And can you blame them? From the infant perspective, there is absolutely nothing going on here. He doesn't know he's going somewhere; he has no concept of travel. All he knows is, he's strapped into this seat in this small enclosure, staring at the back of the seat, and the adults nearby seem to be focused on something that is not him! It's downright offensive, when you think about it.

The true problem infant is the one who does not find car travel to be interesting in the least, yet isn't quite tired enough to doze off. You need to try to get him the rest of the way toward one of those extremes. The dozing scenario will definitely be easier for you, but if you can at least eliminate the mind-bending screams, you will have a better chance of arriving at your destination with some shred of sanity.

Here are some ideas for making the trip bearable:

- **Pictures**—**For very young wild infants, pictures to look at may be useful. You can prop a book or plastic picture holder designed for cars on the seat facing your untamed infant. Or, if your infant loves his own reflection, and you know he does, you can hang a mirror designed for crib use from the back headrest. (This sometimes works for adult passengers, too.)**
- **Movie Time**—**Some parents might opt to entertain their wild infants with portable DVD players designed for travel. There are conflicting views among wild infant parents about letting kids veg out in front of a TV even in the car, but if your infant is super-fussy about car rides, an entertaining baby show might save everyone's brains.**
- **Toys**—**Older infants might enjoy toys on a car ride. You can hook them to the car seat with plastic links so they won't immediately end up on the floor, which is where infants like things to end up.**
- **Timing**—**Another great way to outsmart a car-fussy infant on a long migration is to plan the trip around your baby's normal naptime. Schedule your drive so that the wild creature will be awake in the car seat for up to an hour,**

but not much more. Ideally, he will fall asleep after about an hour, and stay asleep for two hours. Then you can stop and feed the infant, change him, feed yourself if there is time, and return to the car for another hour awake.

☙ If you need to nurse the wild infant or feed him, don't remove him from the car seat while the car is moving. You'll need to plan a stop for this.

SAFARI VACATION

Caring for a wild infant is complicated enough—try not to make it more so by making impractical vacation choices. It's better to take a big vacation before the little creature gets started on crawling or eating solid foods, since these factors will make everything exponentially harder. If you actually do attempt a vacation with your untamed young, you will need to bring so much stuff it will feel like you are transporting an entire Babies "R" Us store with you. Unless, of course, your vacation destination is a Babies "R" Us store. Which, really, isn't such a bad idea.

Here are the things you will need, in addition to whatever adult human needs you think you absolutely need to indulge:

☙ Stroller
☙ Food for the trip, including powdered formula and water
☙ Your breasts, if you're breastfeeding (I can't tell you how many times we have just rolled out of the driveway when I realized I forgot them)
☙ Stocked diaper bag (bring enough diapers for two days; you can buy the rest at your vacation spot)
☙ A favorite toy
☙ A new toy just for the trip—babies love novelty
☙ The good old lovey, which has stood loyally by your wild infant from day one and will now probably be trampled underfoot in the car
☙ Portable crib, sheets, favorite blanket

- ❧ Portable high chair
- ❧ Infant's favorite music (if traveling by car)
- ❧ Babyproofing gadgets and gizmos—You will want to babyproof at least one room of your vacation place if your infant is crawling. You should also bring a pack of outlet covers and a few cabinet locks. Yes, it's going to be like you are bringing a small hardware store with you
- ❧ Health insurance card and doctor's phone number
- ❧ First aid kit
- ❧ Sunscreen

HOTELS

If you're headed on vacation, you're likely staying in a hotel. Here are some ways to make the stay as easy as possible.

- ❧ Minibar—If you are staying at a hotel with a minibar, lock it. If there is no lock, remove the contents and get them out of the infant's reach. Wild infants can party like the best of them, and you don't want yours to raid your stash.
- ❧ Room Location—When you check into a hotel, let them know that your wild infant wakes up at night (and screams). They will probably put you in a room surrounded by vacancies or at the end of a hallway, so he won't wake the other guests. Note: You can't have your infant put in a room far away from you. Trust me on this one.
- ❧ Bedding—If the crib mattress in your hotel room is wrapped in crinkly plastic, put a towel between the mattress and the sheet to make your infant more comfortable and reduce the noise.

BABIES ON A PLANE

If there is one scenario that is possibly more terrifying than the plot of 2006's *Snakes on a Plane*, it is the concept of wild babies on a plane. There is no doubt in my mind that Samuel L. Jackson (and the flight crew of most airlines) would prefer taking on a Boeing full of vipers than a plane full of fussy, squalling wild infants.

So yeah—suffice it to say that wild infants have a certain "reputation" when it comes to air travel, and that reputation is not so good. Wild infants tend to scream for hours, vomit all over their parents, throw things, and have pee and poop emergencies that don't quite make it to the potty in the sky (and no, I don't mean poop heaven).

And there's no one who suffers more from the wild behavior of wild infants on a plane than their parents. It's you who has to figure out how to discreetly change that diaper, even though the bathrooms in planes have zero counter space. It's you who will need to apologize when your wild infant throws Cheerios at a nearby passenger. And it's you who will feel guilty when your wild infant howls in terror during takeoff and landing.

Here are some things to consider when deciding whether to take to the sky with your untamed infant:

It's Harmless

Although air travel with an infant may be difficult for you, it usually poses no physical hazard to your wild infant. Medically speaking, it's fine and dandy for young infants to engage in winged migration. However, some airlines do prohibit infants who are only a few days old. And because planes tend to be a hotbed of germ activity, it might be preferable to wait until your infant is a few months old and has a semifunctional immune system.

Consider the Timing

Think about your untamed infant's temperament at different points in her daily schedule. Is she an evening fusser, requiring long walks or hours of rocking to calm down? Then hold off on booking that evening flight. Is she the type who sleeps all night long? Maybe you can try a red-eye. Although if your infant surprises you and screams through the night, you can expect the eyes of your sleepless fellow passengers to glow red with malice and ill will toward you.

Get Baby a Seat

Yes, a wild infant can fly free or very cheaply if he sits on your lap, so it might be tempting to purchase tickets for adult humans only. However, this is generally not a very good idea, both in terms of your infant's safety and whatever small amount of sanity you have left. Go ahead and pony up for an airplane seat for your wild infant. Here's why:

- ❧ **Safety—If the airplane should hit turbulence or have an accident, your untamed infant can be severely injured if she isn't strapped into her car seat. That's right—a car seat on an airplane. Yes, wild infants can fly in so-called "car seats," as long as they are FAA-approved and "certified for use in motor vehicles and aircraft." This is something to consider when buying your wild infant's first conveyance. In addition to safety, the seat adds a bit of extra familiarity in a situation that, to your wild infant, will seem very strange. (You might need to show proof that your car seat is FAA-approved. Ideally, it will be right on the label, but if not, you might have to whip out the instruction manual.)**
- ❧ **Annoyance—Having a spot guaranteed for your wild baby's car seat can make the difference between a difficult airplane flight and hell in the sky. (With a car seat, you will have the option of putting the infant down if she falls asleep. You'll also have half a chance of being able to lower your tray table and actually ingest food yourself—emphasis on the word "half.")**
- ❧ **Window Seat—When you buy an airplane seat for your infant, be sure it is a window seat, since that is sometimes**

the only place the car seat can be used, depending on the size and layout of the plane. Also, it goes without saying that you don't want your wild infant seated in an exit row where she'll be responsible for saving the whole plane in the event of an emergency.

- ❦ Aisle *and* Window—If you decide *not* to buy an extra seat for your untamed infant, your best bet is to ask for an aisle and a window seat. If Lady Luck is rooting for you, the center seat will remain unoccupied. If not, you still have an excellent chance that whoever has that seat will not be the type of person who enjoys being sandwiched between an insane wild infant and her parental figure. Ask this individual to switch with you.

- ❦ Bulkheads?—Someone might have recommended that you ask for a bulkhead row, but your chances of that are slim unless your partner or your wild infant is a frequent flier business traveler. Airlines tend to give out bulkhead seats to "good" customers, and families with regurgitating infants are usually not in that category.

- ❦ Front Third—Try to get a seat in the front third of the plane. Some planes have extra legroom for passengers in the front of the plane. This might make all the difference in whether you will be able to shimmy down to pick up a dropped lovey after your wild infant tosses it for the eighteenth time. If you can't get a seat toward the front, seek out one in the last few rows. This gives you a little bit of pacing room, at least.

Plane Tips for Wild Infant Parents

Okay, so if you feel it is necessary to take your wild infant along on an airplane trip, there are some things you can do to make it a little bit easier on the wild one, yourself, and your fellow travelers. You will still need to bring a bunch of extra gear, make a bunch of high-maintenance requests, and plan for all kinds of wacky contingencies. That's just the nature of this beast we call "infant." The best-case scenario is that your extensive preparation and pain-in-the-butt special requests will make for a less horrible flight than you could have had.

Here are some ideas for making your trip more tolerable.

Gate-Check the Stroller

The idea behind this is that you can push your wild infant all the way down the boarding ramp, and then unload the stroller just outside the door to the plane. Tell the person checking boarding passes that you want a gate check. They will give you a special tag, which you will affix to the stroller when you leave it behind. Unless there is some horrible baggage snafu, the stroller will be returned to you as you leave the plane at your destination. You are just going to have to trust in all those "object permanence" lessons you taught your infant through play. The stroller went away, but it will be back. The stroller went away, but it will be back. Keep repeating it.

Bring Extra Formula

There are two reasons your untamed infant should drink as much as possible on the plane. One, it is dehydrating to travel by plane, and two, the sucking motion of the jaw can help protect your wild infant's ears from pressure or "popping." Bring a lot of water with you if you are using powdered formula. Airline security rules don't allow liquids in sizes over 3 ounces, but breastmilk, formula, and juice are cool if you have the requisite infant to go with them. Bottles of water aren't allowed through the security gates, but you can buy them once you've gotten through and add them to your infant's bottle. So, are we still thinking this trip's worth it?

Consider Preboarding

It is much easier to get yourself, your infant, and your private inventory of baby stuff situated before the stampede of wild travelers comes barreling down the aisle trying to cram past you and your young. For some reason, preboarding of young kids is not offered as often these days, so you're going to have to make another special request. **Note**: Some adult humans are not especially comfortable with making special requests. These humans cringe at the idea of asking for special dressing on the side of their salad, baked potatoes instead of scalloped potatoes, and water with a wedge of lime instead of lemon, with the wedge removed after spritzing, please. If you happen to be one of these people, you really should wait until your untamed infant is more civilized to take her on a plane, which is to say, quite a bit older. Like, at least five.

Getting back to preboarding: ask if you can do that. If you are traveling alone with your infant, you will need to beg. I can only hope that at this point, after you've gate-checked your stroller, requested a bulkhead seat, and put your breast secretions through security, you have abandoned your shyness and are embarrassment-proof.

Heat Up Bottles with Barf Bags

You probably never knew how wonderfully versatile an airplane barf bag could be, unless you're MacGyver or maybe Martha Stewart. If you need to heat up a bottle on a plane, fill a barf bag halfway with hot water (the flight attendants have it for tea), put the bottle in the water, and let it sit.

Suckle During Takeoff and Landing

Because you do not have a bird as a wild infant, she will not be used to significant changes in altitude. As stated, sucking and swallowing helps spare your wild infant ear pressure and discomfort during takeoff and landing. If you are lucky enough to have a sleeping infant during takeoff, let her stay that way. If she's sleeping during landing, though, you need to wake her up. The logic here is that pressure problems are the worst during landing. Besides, once you reach your destination, there's a fair chance your infant will wake up anyway. If she rejects your offer of food, use an eyedropper to put drops of water, juice, or milk in her mouth. This swallowing will clear her ears. Or, she may opt to clear her ears the old-fashioned way: by screaming bloody murder. Hopefully, she'll do this only during landing, when the whole ordeal is almost over.

Keep the Maternal Parent Hydrated

Yes, it's good for everyone, even adults, to drink plenty of water on an airplane flight. But do you seriously think this is about you and your comfort and/or well-being? Ha, ha! No, of course not; if you are a nursing female, you need to get that water in you to prevent the milk factory from coming to a screeching halt. Bring a sport water bottle and ask to have it refilled. This is a lot easier for you to handle while simultaneously tending to your squirmy wild infant than a 4-ounce plastic glass that you have to keep on the tray table.

Bring Extra Clothes

If your wild infant explodes disgusting gunk from either end of her body, the chances are good that her clothes are not the only ones that will get soiled. Keep a change of clothes (for you) and plastic grocery bags (for the ick) in your carry-on. Hmm, this isn't too much for you to remember, is it?

Bring a Favorite Toy

You can also "create your own" toys. For example, you can make puppets out of the barf bags. No one will think you're crazy at all. And don't worry about needing the bags for their functional purpose. If your infant is going to barf, she's going to do it on your face!

Bring Earplugs

Seriously, if people start giving you hateful looks because of your squalling infant, you can offer the earplugs around. If nothing else, it will show that you're able to make light of your situation. You might even get one of those miserable passengers to crack a smile. Hopefully, your infant will not follow this up by pelting them with Baby Bullet storage cups. It's no fun to take a bullet from a baby, even if the bullet is filled with strained carrots and mashed turkey.

Have a Diaper Plan

It is not easy to find a place to change a wild infant's diaper on a plane. The bathrooms tend to be small, wet, and sticky (just like your infant), and few are equipped with foldout changing tables. If you have a row to yourself, you should change the wild infant's diaper on your seats. If you open the diaper and it is a real stink bomb, smile remorsefully at any nearby passengers and get that thing into a barf bag as quickly as possible (don't use that one as a puppet, okay?). If you don't have a row to yourself, change the wild infant on the floor at the rear of the plane. Try to duck down and stay out of the path of people walking by. The floor will probably be kind of gross, so put a blanket or two on the floor before you roll out your changing pad. Again, a sheepish shrug or smile might help smooth over a gagworthy smell.

Another approach to the infant waste dilemma is to put liberal amounts of diaper cream and a superabsorbent diaper on your wild infant just prior to boarding. Then, cross your fingers and hope that her poop doesn't hijack the plane.

Avoid Changing Planes

If at all possible, definitely try to get a direct flight for yourself and your traveling wild infant. If you're flying alone with an infant and her entourage of stuff, it might be impossible to race from gate to gate. So try Special Request No. 1,500—call the airline and see if they can get you a chauffeured electric cart.

Be Nice to Airline Staff

No matter what else goes on, remember this: As warm and friendly as your flight attendant may seem, with her friendly greetings and her little cans of V8 and her smilingly pantomimed safety instructions, she is not exactly the BFF of the adult human traveling with a wild infant. She has a job to do, and it involves keeping a whole plane of people reasonably content, calm, and orderly. It does not involve making sure you find a place to change your infant's diaper, helping you stow his car seat in the overhead bin, or mushing up vegetables for him to vomit. It is important to remember this, because there will probably be about a thousand times you will feel like you need to seek his or her assistance. But there's only so much you can count on from this person, especially if the flight is crowded.

You might get lucky and have a flight attendant who remembers what it is like to travel with a feral infant and shows you some mercy, but you can't rely on this.

A Day at the Beach

The wild baby tends to find much delight and fascination near vast bodies of water and in sand-covered environments with lots of noise. For this reason, your little creature will probably fit right in on your beach vacation. However, it is important to remember that the shore isn't your creature's primary habitat, so he'll need special protection from the sun and surf. In addition, he will probably require some extra gear to keep him amused, clean, and full.

Here's how to transport your young to the sea and home again without any major disasters.

Sunscreen

Wild infants under six months of age should only have sunscreen on limited areas, such as their faces or backs of their hands. Your first approach should be to shield the newborn infant with protective clothing or shade, with sunscreen as a second resort. UV-protective onesie time!

When he's old enough, choose a sunscreen labeled "Broad Spectrum" to guard against both UVB and UVA rays, with an SPF of at least 15. Untamed infants have very delicate, vulnerable skin, and serious burns in early childhood can be very damaging.

For sensitive body parts, such as the nose, cheeks, tops of ears, and shoulders, you can try a sunscreen or sunblock with zinc oxide or titanium dioxide. Do a "patch test" of these sunscreens before slathering it on your wild infant. This means put a dab on the inside of the baby's arm and cover it with a Band-Aid. Check the skin after 20 minutes and after 24 hours. If there are red blotches or bumps, you shouldn't use that brand on your miniature human.

JUNGLE
PLAYDATE

As prolific at breeding as rabbits are known to be, they aren't such champs at actually caring for their young. According to NationalGeographic.com, rabbit moms ditch their babies in burrows immediately after they're born. Mom then comes back to feed them for a whopping two minutes a day for their first twenty-five days. "Oh, and then after twenty-five days, she has more time to give, right?" you're probably thinking. Nope. After their twenty-five-day childhoods, they're on their own. Have a nice life, kids!

In Mom Rabbit's defense, she might be avoiding the rabbit's nest so that predators won't discover where the nest is located. Don't go getting any ideas, human moms—no one wants to eat your baby! By the way, Mrs. Rabbit's parenting book, *The Two-Minute Mom*, is being released later this year. Don't buy it!

- -

Clothing

Dress your untamed infant in lightweight cotton clothes that cover the upper and lower limbs, even if you are also using sunblock. Use a hat with a brim that goes all the way around the infant head, and covers the back of the neck, too. You should also make an attempt to place 100 percent ultraviolet filtration sunglasses on your infant's face. He may throw them off immediately, but he might think he looks like a little rock star in them and wear them all day. Don't use play or toy sunglasses—without 100 percent UV filtration, they actually do more harm than good. Although they do look super cool.

Bring an Umbrella

Bring or rent a beach umbrella and keep your feral one in the shade as much as possible. You might even want to get off the beach entirely during the middle of the day, when the sun's rays are most powerful and damaging. Really, you and your adult human partner could probably stand a little shade, too. What's that smell? I think it's your brain boiling!

Toys

If your wild offspring is old enough to grasp a toy in his hand, bring a bucket and shovel. He might not have a clue as to how to play with them just yet, but he will greatly enjoy watching you dump water and sand with them. Also, if you construct a beautiful and elaborate sandcastle, he will gleefully and immediately destroy it. A wild infant's keenest desire is to throw things on the ground, or, if the thing is already on the ground, to completely level and destroy it. So these games will be right up his alley.

Bring Swim Diapers

Pack plenty of diapers and swim diapers. Swim diapers don't contain superabsorbent gels like regular diapers, so they don't fill up with water and explode. Not exploding is nice, at least by your standards (your wild infant might disagree). Swim diapers hold poop decently, but are not so great with pee. You will want to change your feral creature's diapers fairly often, both to prevent diaper rash and to keep our oceans clean.

Bring Extra T-Shirts

Your infant should be wearing a T-shirt while splashing around in the surf to protect him from the sun. Then you should change him into a dry shirt. This might need to be repeated a few times, so pack a lot of T-shirts.

Bring Water

Bring extra fluids to keep the nursing female and the wild infant hydrated. Male adults, whatever.

Dealing with Sand

Use a cornstarch-based baby powder or actual cornstarch to remove sand. This is more effective than rinsing the untamed infant with water.

It is very likely that your wild infant will taste, and even eat, a fair amount of sand. This is not a concern. It'll just go right through him and pass out the other end. It will be like a little mini-beach in his diaper.

Immersion

Feel free to dip your wild infant's toes in the water. But don't bring him all the way in until he has mastered the challenging task of being able to support his own head. Also, don't bring an untamed infant into water that is colder than 84°F, because infants are more vulnerable to hypothermia. To be safe, don't keep your wild infant even in warm water for more than half an hour.

To Float or Not to Float

While swimming in a pool with your feral young, you can use a tube made specifically for infants, with straps between the legs. Or you can use a life vest. Whichever you choose, don't think they are a substitute for you staying within reach. Stay with your wild infant at all times in the water.

Chapter 14

COMMUNICATION ACROSS SPECIES

You might think that having elaborate conversations with a wild infant is kind of like trying to talk in underwater squeaks and whistles to a baby whale. Everything's kind of garbled, low frequency, and sad—you have no idea if you're making any sense, and your wild infant is looking at you like she wishes you would shut your blowhole. Plus, those ten lingering pounds of baby weight are totally making you feel like Shamu.

But don't give up! Talking to your wild infant is one of the most important things you can do for her intellectual development. Your untamed infant listened to you while she floated happily in the womb, and she is quite familiar with the sound of your voice. Talking to your feral creature, as well as singing or reading children's books, are excellent ways to help her develop language. It's very likely that the first words she says will be an imitation of something you said. Let's hope it's not #*@ %@#*, or *#@$ *& $)(&%. Those wouldn't be very nice first words.

CHECK OUT THE BIG BRAIN ON BABY!

Even though your wild infant will be more or less incapable of taking an IQ test or giving any measurable indication of his intelligence, infant zoologists have learned a great deal about what goes on underneath that soft spot on his skull. Infant intellectual milestones come in leaps and bounds during the first year, even though your wild infant probably has very little to show for it other than a dazzling ability to throw things. You might mock it now, but when he's an Olympic discus-throwing champion you will humbly apologize.

Here are some of the amazing feats of the mind your wild infant will achieve within his first year of life:

- **Interest in Others**—At two months, wild infants become interested in things besides themselves and their adult female parent. This is a good time to break out the toys and the long-suffering lovey. This is excellent news for you, because it means your infant can be distracted when he descends into a fussiness funk. It's also excellent news because it probably means your kid won't grow up to be a total egomaniac.

- **Quantity**—Between three and four months of age, your infant can begin to grasp that three objects are more than two objects (he will subsequently begin to wonder why the female parent does not have three breasts instead of two). At about four months, he learns to expect regular events. Like when the female parent takes out her nursing pillow or breast, he might propose a toast.

- **Preferences**—At about four months of age, he will begin to prefer some people or toys to others. Like when daddy gets home from work, he might get all excited, even though the *Maternicus martryius* has been slaving and producing breastmilk for him all day long. What a little ingrate—just saying.

- **Gazing**—At five months of age, he will learn to follow another person's gaze—if you glance toward the TV, he will too. (Of course, if you don't glance toward the TV, he still might.)

- **Mirror Awareness**—At roughly six to nine months of age, he will start to realize that the face he sees in the mirror is his own, not some rival creature out to usurp his place in the pecking order (that comes later—it's called a sibling). Once he gets this, it will be love at first sight.

☙ Object Permanence—At about eight to nine months of age, he will start to understand object permanence— that when you leave the room or a cherished object is not visible, you and it continue to exist. (You can test this by hiding a toy under a blanket. Before your infant understands object permanence, he won't even look under there to find it.) You might have to revisit this lesson down the road when the first pet goldfish dies. Um, yeah, so Mr. Snorkles still exists, but in another dimension, as pure energy . . .

☙ Goal Setting—By eight or nine months, your wild infant will have some serious lessons under his belt. He will be able to set a goal, make a plan to carry it out, and ignore distractions while carrying out the plan. Whoa, look out, world! Of course, the goal will be something like "throw my mush cereal on the floor," the plan to accomplish it will be "dump it vigorously," and the distraction he ignores will be "the adult parent attempting to prevent my messy and defiant behavior." Still, though, all the elements of future achievement are in place. Congrats, kid!

How to Talk to a Wild Human Who Cannot Answer You

When your wild infant was first born, her sense of hearing was her most developed sense. She's been listening to you since before she even entered the world. She knows the sound of your voice, and she likes to hear you talk. If you are the wild female human in your household, this is super good news. It means you have not only a captive audience (like your male partner may or may not be for you), but also a willing one!

Whether you are the mom or the dad, you should talk your untamed infant's ear right off. It might feel weird at first, but before long, it will feel pretty natural. And then, before you know it, she'll be answering you! (Not long after that, she'll be talking back to you. But let's not fast forward that far, shall we?)

Here are some language tips for starting the conversation with a wild infant:

- 🐾 **Avoid Baby Talk—There's really no need to use cutesy nonsense words with your untamed infant, although occasional lapses are only human. But in general, you should say "blanket" instead of "blankie," and "water" instead of "wawa." (I know, I was the one who used the term "lovey." But what else do you suggest? "Lover?") By using actual words, you are letting your infant hear the various sounds of her actual language.**

- 🐾 **Avoid Pronouns—In the beginning, your untamed baby will have some trouble getting her mind around pronouns, so instead of saying "I," "you," or "he," just say, "Mommy," "Emma," or "Daddy." Your infant must first learn that everything and everyone has a precise name that's just for them. It might take a while for her to then grasp that all females can be called "she," and everyone on the planet can be called "you." Baby steps, so to speak!**

- 🐾 **Narrate—One way to keep the words flowing while you are with your wild infant is to pretend you are the narrator of a documentary film starring your wild infant. Describe everything that happens. You can say, for example, "Mama is taking off Emma's pajamas. One snap, two snaps, three snaps. Oh, look! There is Emma's belly. Now Mama is taking off Emma's diaper! Oh, my! Look at the feces Emma has deposited in her diaper! My goodness!"**

If your infant responds with any noise at all, even an extremely loud diaper explosion, act like she has answered you. Wait for her to finish her "comment," and then respond. These are the beginnings of her conversation skills. Then change the diaper.

JUNGLE
PLAYDATE

Ah, it's tough to be nurturing and affectionate when your body is covered in flesh-impaling quills! Yet in spite of this, the porcupine mom manages to do a decent job with her little porcupettes (yes, that's their supercute name) until they're about two years old. At that point, she pretty much abandons them, but give her some credit! She goes through a lot just to have them. The mating process, for example, is pretty nasty—and not even in the, um, prickly way you might imagine. According to Neatorama. com, the male porcupine, that charmer, seduces the female by walking up to her, standing on his hind legs, and dousing her with urine from head to foot. If this doesn't sound awesome enough, the end result is getting to give birth to the equivalent of little pincushions—yay!

Luckily for mom, the baby's quills don't harden until a few hours after birth. Oh, and as for porcupine dad? If he didn't have you at *golden hose-down*, you know you're going to swoon over the fact that he's also a *total absentee dad* to the porcupettes. Talk about a real "prick!"

FROM SCREAMS TO "NO"

You may remember the "Baby-Cries-to-Human Dictionary" in the earlier chapters of this guide. This dictionary loosely translates the various infant cries, which are, indeed, a wild infant's first mode of communication.

As your wild infant grows and develops, from baby teeth to solid poop to finger foods, his communication skills also progress continually. He goes from generic loud cries and screams to slightly different loud cries and screams to coos and babbles. Then he progresses to the word "No" and "It's not fair" and "Can I borrow the car?"

Okay, that was a bit of a sped-up summary. But they really do learn fast!

Here are some of the language milestones of wild infants. Some of them you've already experienced, while others are in your near future:

🐾 **Newborn—A newborn infant pretty much just cries. And also screams. These cries and screams really don't sound all that different from each other. They might vary in volume, but only from "loud" to "louder."**

🐾 **One to Two Months—At this age, the cries begin to sound different, and can be interpreted to mean hunger, pain, exhaustion, frustration, and poop. It is not always possible to tell the difference between these sounds, but there have been some scientific theories (see the Baby-Cries-to-Human Dictionary).**

🐾 **Six Weeks to Two Months—The wild infant begins at this point to make cooing sounds, or sometimes just ooh-ing sounds. He's working primarily on vowels at this point, since they are easier and more similar to plain old cries (just think of the typical cry, it's something like, "AAAAAAAAAAAAH" not "kanakazuqualmk").**

- ❧ **Four to Five Months**—At this point, your wild infant understands his name, even if he can't quite say it. And he definitely can't say it if his name happens to be "Kanakazuqualmk."

- ❧ **Four to Eight Months**—At this point, the wild infant begins to babble, which essentially means he is introducing consonants into his lexicon. Unfortunately for female human parents, the consonant D comes much more naturally than M for some infants, and so you might hear "Dada" before "Mama." Don't take it personally; it's all about laziness (as are many things Dad-related).

- ❧ **Nine Months**—At this age, the infant can understand the word "No." This does not mean he will obey that instruction, of course. It means that before long, he'll be able to use it to disobey you. Uh-oh.

- ❧ **Eight to Fourteen Months**—The infant begins to point. For now, that's an awesome milestone. Later, after you've congratulated him on it for a good year and a half, you'll have to tell him it's sort of rude.

- ❧ **Ten Months**—At this point, your wild infant is able to respond physically to a spoken request, like "Bring me the ball." But don't be alarmed if he doesn't bring you the ball—he just might not feel like it.

- ❧ **Ten to Twelve Months**—The baby babbles without repeating syllables. That's kind of refreshing, right? Nobody wants to hear the same syllables over and over, unless your name is Dada.

- ❧ **Ten to Twelve months**—Your wild infant might speak his first words. Hopefully, they won't be "Eff off, lady."

RHYTHM AND RHYME

Yes, there will be times when the adult/infant conversation runs dry. You might just run out of things to say. Well, that's why we have nursery rhymes. In fact, when I run out of things to say to my adult human partner, I simply recite a nursery rhyme to him. And then he says something like, "You're really creepy," or "You need to get some help," and voila! The conversation is up and running again!

For wild infants, it can be especially enjoyable to chant interactive nursery rhymes, in which you can use your baby's fingers and toes to tap out the rhythm. Infants love their digits; they're like little wiggly toys that are attached to their bodies. Plus, they probably can sense that as adults, they will be spending many long hours giving the "thumbs up" on Facebook.

Anyway, here are some fun finger/toe-type rhymes to enjoy with the wild infant in your house.

Finger/Toes Song

These are the baby's fingers (touch fingers),
These are the baby's toes (touch toes),
This is the baby's belly button (touch belly button),
Round and round it goes (draw circles on belly).

This is really little more than an anatomy lesson. Hopefully, your wild infant won't be too bitter about the reference to her belly button. After all, it was once the source of total passive nutrition and oxygenated blood, and will be the future site of a rebellious barbell stud piercing. For now, though, it's just a super little whirly circle! Whee!

This Little Piggy

This little piggy went to market,
This little piggy stayed home,
This little piggy had roast beef,
This little piggy had none.
And this little piggy went wee-wee-wee-wee,
All the way home.

Okay, this rhyme is about as sick and twisted as they get. What are pigs doing, eating roast beef? It verges on cannibalism. But wild infants will enjoy the "wee-wee-wee," so it can't be that bad. I guess.

Pat-a-Cake

Pat-a-cake, Pat-a-cake,
Baker's man,
Bake me a cake as fast as you can.
Roll it, and pat it,
And mark it with a B,
And put it in the oven
For baby and me.

This rhyme is cute, although most people say "patty cake," which doesn't make sense as an instruction to the baker's man. Also, all of these rhymes about food seem to be begging for a future eating disorder. I'm not concerned if you're not!

BABY SIGN LANGUAGE

While you're exploring your wild infant's verbal capabilities, you can also begin to introduce what is known as "baby sign language." You can start teaching your untamed infant some signs when he is about seven or eight months old. A good time to try this is when the untamed creature is sitting in his high chair at dinnertime, and his hands are free. Wild infant experts believe that baby sign language not only speeds up the development of spoken language, but also reduces potential meltdowns because the infant can communicate what's irking him. Of course, you probably already know that some of your infant's tantrums could be best expressed by a single middle finger. But we're looking to be a little bit more precise—and classy—than that.

Here are some basic signs you can teach your untamed young during his first year. You can also make up your own—all that matters is that your infant gets it.

All Gone/Empty

Sweep your right hand over your downturned left hand. Be prepared to defend yourself against hungry jaws that don't want to accept that it's all gone or empty.

Down

This one is really self-explanatory. Your infant will totally get it.

All Gone/Empty: Sweep your right hand over your downturned left hand.

Down: Point your index finger downward. Lower your finger a few inches.

Drink

Cup your hand as if holding an invisible glass. Raise it up to your mouth as if drinking. Once again, superintuitive, although maybe less so if your infant is used to suckling a breast rather than using a cup.

Drink: Cup your hand as if holding an invisible glass. Raise it up to your mouth as if drinking.

More

Hold both hands in front of you, with the fingers on each hand held together and thumbs tucked in, forming a loose "O" shape. Bring the fingertips of both hands together in front of you twice. This is one that, once your untamed infant gets it, he will use over and over and over again.

Scared

Place your hands open, fingers spread wide, against the front of your chest. This is useful during those times when you feel scared of your wild infant.

More: Hold both hands in front of you, fingers on each hand held together and thumbs tucked in, forming a loose "O" shape. Bring the fingertips of both hands together in front of you twice.

Scared: Place your hands open, fingers spread wide, against the front of your chest.

Sit

Extend the index and middle fingers of your left hand horizontally in front of your body, palm down. Raise the same fingers on your right and bring them down to rest on your left fingers. I would say you should then sit, but when do you really have time to do that?

Sit: Extend the index and middle fingers of your left hand horizontally in front of your body, palm down. Raise the same fingers on your right hand and bring them down to rest on your left fingers.

Tired

Tilt your head to one side, bring the palm of one hand up to your cheek. Rest your head against your open palm. As a human adult parent, you may as well go around signing this all day.

Tired: Use the sign for bed as shown: Tilt your head to one side. Bring the palm of one hand up to your cheek. Rest your head against your open palm. Or you place your hands palms in, on your shoulders and move them down from your shoulders as you slump.

GOOD READS!

Reading aloud to your wild infant is another excellent way of developing language skills and fostering a love of books. Not to mention, it can be a great way to settle that wild banshee down so that she might fall asleep sometime this year!

Of course, you can read to your untamed infant from baby books, or, if you'd rather, from whatever material interests you (well, except *Fifty Shades of Grey*). When you are reading aloud to your infant, you have a tremendous amount of power—you are processing, visualizing, and interpreting for two. So you can provide your own editorial commentary, and your infant cannot question you! It's never going to be this good again!

Here are some concepts to keep in mind while reading aloud to your wild infant:

🐾 **Discuss**—Talk about the story as you read. Describe the illustrations, and point out any details that relate to your wild infant's environment. (For example: "Look! That doggie is just like Emma's doggie! He is big!" or "How come Goofy wears clothes, stands upright, and talks, while Pluto grovels on all fours and wears a collar? Aren't they both dogs? I don't get it, Emma. Explain it, for the love of God!")

🐾 **Question**—Ask questions about how and why certain events are happening in the story, and then answer your own questions. You're really just verbalizing your thought process and letting your untamed infant hear you thinking aloud.

🐾 **Repeat**—Be willing to read the same book over and over and over, even if you're bored and ready to move on. Infants like repetition, and it helps develop memory and comprehension. So, be ready to say *Goodnight, Moon* for the 100th time.

🐾 **Be a Voiceover Artist**—Reading aloud to your kid lets you bring out your inner actor. Develop different voices for different characters, act out noise and sounds, and exaggerate the pitch of your voice. Improvise and be creative. Then refuse to sign autographs and balk at your zillion-dollar contract. You're a star!

THE SOUND OF MUSIC

While voicing your wild infant's storybooks can bring out your inner actor, singing to your untamed youth can bring out your inner American Idol. Seriously, even if you are really, really terrible, you should sing to your wild infant. He will appreciate it, even if he's giving you the Simon Cowell treatment in his head.

Here are some ideas about how to add music to your wild infant's life:

🐾 Turn on the stereo to listen to music you enjoy. It can be anything—rock, reggae, classical, opera, country, whatever. Your infant will have a primal reaction to the sounds of rhythm and singing and musical instruments. It is ingrained in all human specimens. You really don't have to go and get special kid music (unless you actually want to hear "I love you, you love me" repeated ad nauseam). All of that will come later, when your infant will be able to identify and demand the latest kid hits. For now, you can make him listen to your stuff!

🐾 If you have a wind-up music box (on a mobile, in a stuffed animal, or in a jewelry box), get a lot of use out of that. Use it to entertain your wild infant in the crib or on the changing table. Down the road, your untamed creature will learn to wind it up himself.

🐾 Shake it! One of the first musical instruments your wild baby will play is his rattle. At first, you'll shake it for him, so he becomes familiar with the noise and follows it around with his gaze. At about four months of age, he will be ready to hold the rattle himself. By six months or so, he will start banging rattles together to hear how that sounds. God help you at that point—he will be ready for drums or a tambourine.

🐾 The wild infant in captivity also enjoys the sounds of the other wild animals in the ecosystem. He will enjoy toys or books that enable him to identify different animals based on the sounds they make (a cow says "moo!" and so forth). You can also teach him about animal sounds by imitating familiar animals in your neighborhood (birds, dogs, etc.). It's a jungle out there—let it in!

Chapter 15

WALKING UPRIGHT

Wow, being a wild infant is seriously hard work. Do you think I'm joking? At the same time she's taking on the challenging tasks of learning to eat, drink, smile, laugh, and learn the language, she is also developing the skills to sit up straight, crawl, and eventually walk. It's basically going from being able to do absolutely nothing to being able to do all of the main things humans are equipped to do, all in a fairly short period of time. Whew! I need a nap just thinking about it!

CHILDPROOFING FOR THE MOBILE INFANT

Once your infant has begun crawling or walking, it is officially half-past childproofing o'clock. When that little gal or fellow is on the move, you are going to want your home to be as harmless as a blind baby bunny. (Actually, probably even a blind baby bunny could be a choking hazard if your wild infant is a real weirdo.) You need to protect your untamed young from her own tendency to wreak total havoc.

Here's some insight into the wild infant mentality: when she sees a fork, for example, this is what she will want to do with it, in descending order:

- **Stick it into an electrical socket**
- **Use it to cut electrical wires**
- **Eat it**

- 😼 Use it to cut electrical wires while also trying to eat it
- 😼 Throw it
- 😼 Stick it in her eyes
- 😼 Stick it in her ears
- 😼 Stick it into a moving fan
- 😼 Put it into the microwave on the "popcorn" setting
- 😼 Use it to eat food like a civilized human

Notice how the sensible, appropriate use of the fork was the last thing to cross the wild infant's mind. Likewise, she will view almost all objects in this manner, seeking to exhaust all dangerous and/or warped possibilities before reluctantly settling for the proper usage.

Therefore, you must treat all objects in the home through the eye of a fearless predator, a.k.a. your infant. Here are some starting tips for this endeavor.

In the Kitchen

- 😼 Gather up all poisonous items, from detergent to vitamins, and place them on your highest shelves (you can also lock these cabinets if you will always close the lock).
- 😼 Get rid of your tablecloth and replace it with a set of placemats. Fine dining is pretty much history at this point, anyway. Your wild infant will undoubtedly try to pull down that tablecloth as soon as she can reach it.
- 😼 Secure your trashcans. Put at least one in a locked cabinet, and think before throwing hazardous materials into an accessible trashcan. Wild infants are filthy little creatures, and they love rooting through trash in pursuit of danger.
- 😼 Lock kitchen cabinets and drawers that contain anything dangerous, such as knives. There's almost nothing more frightening than a knife-wielding wild baby.

🐾 Turn pot handles toward the back of the stove when cooking.

In the Bathroom

🐾 Never in your life did you think you would ever need to *lock your toilet*—well, except for that one time you were dating that freakish guy, but let's just block that out, okay? Anyway, your commode has never been a receptacle that anyone has ever been eager to get into. Enter your wild child, who puts the "toy" in "toilet." For your little one, the toilet is an endless bowl of dubious and disgusting fun. You can purchase a lock, and maybe you should.

🐾 The above warning regarding locking cupboards containing poisonous materials in the kitchen applies to the cabinet under the bathroom sink, too.

Living Room/Den

🐾 Put away all glass-topped coffee tables. They're pretty, but to wild infants, they're like horizontal windows to the floor, made to be broken (and jumped off of). They almost always have nice sharp corners that baby's head will find immediately.

🐾 Secure your television so it won't fall if pushed or pulled.

🐾 Block access to floor lamps or other furniture that is easily tipped over. She will tip them.

🐾 Move breakables or other harmful knickknacks out of reach. For untamed infants, "knickknack" sounds a lot like "midday snack."

🐾 Put your beautiful hardcover books on the upper shelves of your bookcase, and stock your lower shelves with baby books. Secure the bookshelf to the wall. Nothing irks a wild infant more than seeing a bookshelf that's still standing upright—they consider it their personal mission to take it down like a forest full of trees (which, considering its wood-and-paper components, it probably is). And babies don't have the vocabulary or the decency to say "Timber!"

In Any Room

🐾 Install window guards.

🐾 Knot any looped blind cords up and out of reach. Wild infants love ropes, cords, and anything with tangling or strangling potential. They get wild ideas about swinging from drape to coffee table to sectional, like some sort of IKEA Tarzan. Your infant is not yet aware enough to understand that swinging is a terrible idea; someone almost always gets hurt. (Just like you told your spouse!)

🐾 If you sew, put away your sewing basket on a high shelf, and unplug and put away your sewing machine after each use. Make sure yarn and knitting needles are similarly stowed in a safe place

🐾 Identify all houseplants and make sure they are nontoxic.

🐾 Put up gates to prevent your infant from having access to the stairs and any rooms you want to keep off-limits. Use gates that screw into the walls rather than pressure gates. Wild infants have a tendency to defiantly fling their insane little bodies against obstacles, and when (not *if*) your wild child hurls herself against a pressure gate, it could very well collapse.

🐾 Cover electrical outlets. Use either caps for unused outlets, or covers that block access to the plug for outlets you use. Remember our little exercise about the fork.

🐾 Regularly hunt for dropped coins or other choking hazards. A penny saved from the gaping maw of a wild infant is a penny earned.

* Don't put your infant in a walker, or if you do, never let her use it around stairs. No explanation needed.

Outside

* If you have a pool, make sure it is solidly fenced and the gate is closed and locked. Hot tubs should be kept closed and locked when not in use. Don't even leave a pail of water unattended. She might try to use it as a hot tub.
* Garden tools should be locked up in a shed or storage box.

JUNGLE PLAYDATE

One of the most fascinating animal dads is actually an animal mom. Wait, what? Yep, in the seahorse household, the male is the one who gets pregnant. After his woman lays a whole bunch of eggs inside him, this highly progressive guy carries up to 1,000 infants in his sizable "baby bump." Oh, and according to Neatorama.com, he's totally monogamous—he's not going to let any other ladies knock him up. Whew! So, Mrs. Seahorse doesn't have to worry about getting DNA tests to prove she's the mama! On the downside, he does occasionally eat a few of the kids, but come on—he's a dude! What did you expect? Overall, he's pretty cool. Although guys: if a woman ever tells you you're "hung like a seahorse," it *might* be a dubious compliment.

- -

MOTORIN'

Motor skills are essential to many human tasks—you probably take this for granted. But your infant has probably watched you doing all your fancy head turning, sitting up, and walking, and thought, "I want to do that someday. That's totally in my five-year plan."

She does a lot better than that—she gets it all done within a year, in most cases. Here are some of the motor skills milestones you will watch this amazing creature achieve:

Head Turn

Your wild infant's very first voluntary muscle movement will probably be the head turn. You will see this in the first few weeks. Not only does this develop neck muscles, it sets the whole "I want to move" thing in motion. Once this Pandora's box has been opened, your child will pretty much want to voluntarily use her muscles for her entire life, whether it means she's stomping away from you in a huff, or whether she's using her hands to draw you a homemade Mother's or Father's Day card. What can I say? That whole moving thing comes with pluses and minuses.

You can encourage your infant's voluntary head turn by lying down next to her until she looks at you. Then jump up and run around her, and lie down on her other side until she looks your way again. Not only will this inspire the head-turn, it will help get you in shape! Whoo!

Mini Pushup

Voluntary muscle movement number two is the "mini pushup," which occurs between two and four months of age. This move requires a little bit of shoulder muscle to achieve. In this milestone, your wild infant uses her arms to lift her shoulders and chest off of the ground, or off your shoulder if she's settled there.

If your untamed baby spends a lot of time on her back or sitting in her infant seat, she might be a little bit late on this milestone. Don't worry. You can practice these pushups by placing her on her belly on the floor and holding a toy in front of and slightly above her head. Now, that's motivation! Drop and give me twenty, baby!

The Swipe and Grab

This next move is one that you might feel like you will see every day for the rest of your life. It's called the swipe and grab, because that is exactly what it is. You will first see the swipe and grab between the ages of two and five months. This is actually tougher than it sounds. To do it, your infant will need to overcome a reflex she was born with, called the tonic neck reflex. This reflex places your infant's arms in a fencing position—one arm extended, the other arm bent, whenever she is on her back with her head to one side. She can't control her hands until she can overcome this reflex and get both hands in front of her. She also has to quit all that fencing that she's been doing with her fancy prep-school friends.

You can encourage the swipe and grab by using a baby gym. These are available for cribs, playing on the floor, and infant seats. To encourage your wild infant to bring both hands together (the baby equivalent of a clap), sit her in her baby chair and play Pat-a-Cake, clapping the rhyme with your own hands and then with hers. After she starts to get the hang of swiping or swatting at objects, grabbing them is a hop, skip, and a jump away. Although, for your wild infant, a hop, skip and a jump would be seriously hard.

Rolling Over

You might not notice when your wild infant first rolls over, but for some untamed offspring, this is actually the first independent motion she will achieve. Give her some credit, will you? You'd be proud of your dog for rolling over!

The roll usually occurs sometime between three and seven months. An infant who spends a lot of time on her stomach might roll over sooner than her non–stomach lying counterparts, and will probably do the front-to-back roll. Infants that like to chillax on their backs will probably roll later, and will roll from their backs to their fronts. This might give your infant a surprising amount of mobility—you might leave the room for half a minute and find your little creature a good distance away from where she was.

You can encourage your infant to roll over by giving her time on her tummy, and you can also try to roll her across the room like a rolling pin. If she doesn't like that, she will let you know by fussing. Or by saying, "C'mon, mom. That's not how I roll."

Sitting Up

This is a voluntary movement that *you* may have forgotten how to do over the past few months. But once your wild infant masters sitting up, she can have her hands free and can entertain herself, which gives you both a lot of freedom. Granted, it's freedom to do laundry or put away dishes, but still, freedom is freedom! You can do "sitting practice" by surrounding your untamed infant with regular pillows or your nursing pillow to keep her balance. She will probably tip over and need rescuing on a regular basis, so don't go anywhere!

Crawling

This will be a big game-changer for you, your wild infant, and the rest of your household. The untamed human offspring generally begins to crawl at between six and twelve months. Some infants prefer to skip this stage and go for the big showstopper, walking. In addition, some of them might have their own unique variations of the crawl. Some might go backward first, or skitter along sideways like a crab. Others might slouch along using only their arms, like an ape, or do an elephant walk, where they amble along on all fours, but use their feet instead of their knees. Don't worry if your infant doesn't do the "classic" hand-and-knee crawl. That's not the only crawl in town, and your infant knows this.

A crawling infant is seriously mobile, much more so than a roller. So maybe worry less about whether she has perfect form, and more about how quickly she's going to try to fill your DVD player with dog food.

BABYPROOFING REMINDER

Once your infant starts crawling, try crawling around the room yourself, seeing the room at her eye level, and identifying potential dangers such as electrical outlets, tangles of cords, and oven cleaners under the sink. You already know what the dangers will be later, once her eye level is five-foot-four or so (you can tell that infant boy down the street is going to grow into a real charmer). For now, though, get down on the ground and look for upholstery nails!

Upright and Out of Sight!

The next thing you can expect of this unbelievably ambitious little creature is for her to pull herself up into a standing position. Once she starts pulling herself upright, at some point between seven to thirteen months, you can expect her to continue doing so obsessively, as though it is her full-time job. She will start pulling up on just about every object in sight. She might even pull up on her crib in the middle of the night and not be able to get down. This is not good. At around this time, you should lower the crib mattress down to the lowest rung in the frame, so your infant doesn't fall out when standing and bending precariously over the railing.

Once your untamed infant has started pulling up, try to teach her how to sit down again. Actually, though, being able to stand up unsupported requires her to be able to use the muscles around her joints and have a sense of balance. Learning to sit back down again teaches this control and balance. And hopefully it also teaches her to sit back down again!

Keep your wild infant barefoot as much as possible to promote her standing attempts. She will feel much more confident if she can feel the floor with her feet. If it's cold and you feel it would be irresponsible to keep her barefoot, use socks that fit well and have no-skid soles. Don't put your wild infant in a walker; not only does it not teach your infant to walk faster, some experts feel it actually delays independent walking. Plus, she will look like a little old lady!

Walking

Once your untamed young is able to stand up, you can fully expect that walking is not far behind. This usually occurs between ten and sixteen months of age. Infants that are heavier might be on the late end of that range, while some really precocious little creatures might try it even earlier. To some degree, it depends on how safe you make her feel, or how overprotective you are. Don't be fearful and project your fears onto your wild infant. Yes, wild infants might fall, but they are unlikely to be seriously injured. Relax, wild ma or dad—you have successfully gotten your wild infant to walk like a human!

Don't be overly concerned if you think your infant is walking funny—she just got started, after all! Some infants might walk with a "duck walk," with their legs spread wide apart and toes turned out like a duck's. A lot of other infants are naturally pigeon-toed, and some infants have thighs or shins that tilt a little bit. Other untamed offspring might seem to always be walking on tiptoes. If you have a tiptoer, check with your pediatrician for tight muscles. But it's a lot more likely that she just likes walking that way. And look, just about any way a wild infant walks is going to be cute, so don't be a jerk about it! Who ever said your walk was so perfect?

Conclusion

YEAR ONE, IN THE BOOKS

Once your wild infant starts walking around, it's only a hop, skip, and a jump to toddlerhood (um, not a literal, hop, skip, or jump, babies—don't go getting ideas!).

Do you know what that means, parents? It means you've gotten through most—or all—of Year One, with your wild infant safe and thriving, and your sanity (mostly) intact! How amazing is that?

Give yourself a pat on the back—you've survived this journey into the unknown wilderness of the Baby Kingdom, and you've emerged with a whole new set of skills—and a pretty adorable new family member. You might even see a little bit of yourself in this crazy little mammal, and have a new perspective on human nature at its wildest.

Ironically, they say that wild infants have a decidedly "taming" effect on their parents. What nonsense that is! Now go celebrate your successful year with a family-friendly dinner, a bit of SpongeBob (hey, they have some cool guest stars on that show! Can you say *David Bowie*?), and an exhausted passout on the couch at 8:17 P.M. You wild thing, you!

Appendix

RESOURCES

BOOKS

Borden, Marian Edelman and Schonwald, Alison D. *The Everything® Baby's First Year Book, 2nd Edition.* Avon, MA: F+W Media, Inc., 2010.

Bowers, Ellen, PhD. *The Everything® Guide to Raising a Toddler.* Avon, MA: F+W Media, Inc., 2011.

Fredregill, Suzanne, CBE, and Ray Fredregill. *The Everything® Breastfeeding Book, 2nd Edition.* Avon, MA: F+W Media, Inc., 2010.

Iannelli, Vincent. *The Everything® Father's First Year Book, 2nd Edition.* Avon, MA: F+W Media, Inc., 2010.

Huggins, Kathleen. *The Nursing Mother's Companion: Revised Edition.* Boston: Harvard Common Press, 2005.

La Leche League International. *The Womanly Art of Breastfeeding: Seventh Revised Edition.* New York: Penguin, 2004.

Meek, Joan Younger, and Sherrill Tippins. *The American Academy of Pediatrics New Mother's Guide to Breastfeeding.* New York: Bantam, 2005.

Pantley, Elizabeth. *The No-Cry Sleep Solution: Gentle Ways to Help Your Baby Sleep Through the Night*. New York: McGraw-Hill, 2002.

Sears, Martha. *The Breastfeeding Book: Everything You Need to Know about Nursing Your Child from Birth Through Weaning*. Boston: Little, Brown, 2003.

Simpson, Theresa R. *The Everything® Baby Sign Language Book with CD*. Avon, MA: F+W Media, Inc., 2008.

WEBSITES

American Academy of Pediatrics
www.aap.org

American Baby Magazine
www.americanbaby.com

BabyCenter.com
www.babycenter.com

Centers for Disease Control and Prevention
www.cdc.gov

U.S. Consumer Product Safety Commission
www.cpsc.gov

National Association for the Education of Young Children
www.naeyc.org

Parenting and *Baby Talk* Magazines
www.parenting.com

Parenting Section, iVillage.com
www.parenting.ivillage.com

INDEX

Acetaminophen, 160, 167
Airplane travel, 205–14
Air quality, 11–12
Allergies and intolerances, 12, 55,
    82, 110, 112, 117–18
    symptoms of, 124–25
    testing new foods for, 119
Alligators, 15
Allomothers, 133
American Academy of Pediatrics
    (AAP), 19, 40, 48, 82, 105, 125,
    158, 165
Anger, 46, 183
Apgar scores, 18–19
Aspirin, avoiding, 160, 165
Asthma, 12
Automobile travel, 36–37, 202–4

Baby foods
    homemade, 113, 118–19
    organic, 119–20
    reading labels on, 125–27
Baby powder, 105, 217
Babyproofing, 10–14, 205, 245. See
    also Childproofing; Safety
Baby wipes, 102, 107
Bag Balm, 105
Bathing, 135–43, 160
Bath toys, 136, 143
Beach, visits to, 214–17
Belly button care, 146–47
Belly hold, 21
Bisphenol A (BPA), 78
Blanket safety, 9
Blood (in body fluids), 92–93
Bottle-feeding, 77–89, 209. See also
    Bottles; Formula
    avoiding solids in, 116
    bloopers, 85–87
    colic and, 52
    gadgets for, 79–81
    instructions for, 87–89
Bottles
    finding the right, 77–79
    heating with barf bags, 210
    keeping hot during outings, 196
Boys, 18, 100, 102, 103, 144–46
Breast augmentation, breastfeeding
    and, 77
Breastfeeding, 55–75. See also

Breast pumps/breastmilk
    benefits of, 55–56
    colic and, 52
    contraindications for, 77
    after a C-section, 61–63
    frequency of, 60
    gear for, 66–68
    how-to, 56–59
    suckling issues, 69–71
    tips for, 59–61
    types of feeders, 63–66
    urination and, 91
Breastmilk jaundice, 24
Breast pumps/breastmilk, 63, 67,
    71–75, 81, 86
Breathing problems, 163
Bumper pads, avoiding, 32
Burping, 61, 89

Caesarian section (C-section), 17,
    61–63
Caput, 22
Carbon monoxide detectors, 12
Car seats, 8–9, 207–8
Centers for Disease Control, 19
Cheerios, 131
Childproofing, 237–41. See also
    Babyproofing; Safety
Choking hazards, 31, 125, 131, 154,
    176, 240
Circumcision, 144–45
Cocoa butter, 106
Colic, 21, 51–52, 82
Colostrum, 60
Communication, 219–35
    intellectual milestones, 219–21
    language milestones, 224–25
    reading aloud, 233–34
    sign language, 228–33
    talking to babies, 221–23
Constipation, 56, 112
Cornstarch, 217
Coughing, 164
Coxsackie, 167–68
Cradle cap, 148–49
Cradle/rock hold, 20, 57
Crawling, 244–45
Cribs, 8
Crying, 43–52, 163
    techniques for easing, 46–48

types of, 44–46

Dairy products, 52, 122–23. *See also* Milk
Defecation, 45, 56, 93–94, 110, 160. *See also* Constipation; Diarrhea; Meconium
Dehydration, 161, 162, 163. *See also* Hydration
Diabetes, 55
Diaper bag, packing, 193–94
Diaper rash, 95, 104–7
Diapers, 95–103
    changing on airplanes, 212
    changing tips, 102–3
    cloth, 96, 97–99
    disposable, 92, 96, 97, 100–101
    gear for changing, 95
    instructions for use, 101–2
    swim, 216
Diarrhea, 56, 123, 161–62
Drinking practice, 127–29

Ear infections, 12, 86, 157
Ear popping (on airplanes), 209, 210–11
Egrets, 53
Elephants, 133
Elimination, 91–107. *See also* Defecation; Diapers; Urination
Embryonic diapause, 194
Emotional milestones, 181–85
Emperor Penguin, 83–84
Eye inflammation/discharge, 164

Falls, 30
Feeding, 109–32. *See also* Baby foods; Bottle-feeding; Breastfeeding; Finger foods; Restaurants; Solid foods
    adding a daytime, 38
    focal, 41–42
    foods to avoid, 131
    sharing nighttime, 38
Ferberizing, 39–40
Fever, 157–60, 163, 168
Fifth disease, 167, 168–69
Finger foods, 129–32, 198–99
Floppiness, 162
Fluoride, 155
Focal feeding, 41–42
Formula, 81–85, 209. *See also* Bottle-feeding
    hypoallergenic, 83

mixing and preparing, 84–85
Fruits, 132

Galactosemia, 82–83
Games, 176–78
Gas, 21
Gates, 29, 240
Gazing, 220
Giant Pacific octopus, 39
Girls, 18, 92–93, 102, 146
Goal setting, 221
Grooming and hygiene, 135–51. *See also* Bathing; Hair care; Nail trimming; Private parts (hygiene)

Hair care, 138, 147–49
Head molding, 22
Head turn, 242
Healthy Sleep Habits, Happy Child (Weissbluth), 41
Hepatitis B vaccine, 19
Hiking, 201–2
Holding babies, 19–21
Hotels, 205
Hunger, crying and, 45
Hydration, 60, 160, 209, 211, 217. *See also* Dehydration
Hydrocortisone cream, 105
Hypothyroidism, 19

Ibuprofen, 160
Illness, 157–69. *See also* Medications; specific disorders
    breastfeeding and reduced risk of, 55
    causes for concern, 160–62
    crying and, 45, 163
    signs of in older infants, 163–66
    supplies for, 164
Immunoglobulin A (IgA), 110
Intellectual milestones, 219–21
Iron, dietary, 81, 113, 124

Japanese Cardinal Fish, 30–31
Jaundice, 23–24
Juices, 121, 129

Kangaroos, 194

Lactose intolerance, 82
Language milestones, 224–25
Laughter, 182–83
Lead, 12–14, 176
Letdown, 71, 72

Loveys, 37, 40, 185
Lullabies, 36

Marmosets, 161
Mastitis, 70
Meats, 122–23
Meconium, 60, 94, 102
Medications
   administering, 165–67
   for colic, 51–52
   for newborns, 19
   for post-C-section pain, 62
Medina, Kol, 99
Meningitis, 163
Microwave use and
   contraindications, 74, 85, 86, 106,
   119
Milk, 82–83, 124. *See also* Dairy
   products
Milk ducts, clogged, 70
Mini pushup, 242–43
Mirror awareness, 220–21
Mommy Wars, 48, 95–96
Motor skills, 242–43
Movies, attending with baby,
   199–200
Music, 234–35

Nail trimming, 149–51
Naked mole rat, 148
Naps, 35, 41
Nipples (bottle), 78–79, 84
Nipple soreness, 68–69
The No-Cry Sleep Solution (Pantley),
   41
Nursery rhymes, 225–28

Object permanence, 177, 178, 221

Pacifiers, 48, 80
Pain, crying and, 45
Paint, lead in, 12–13
Pantley, Elizabeth, 41
Pasta, 132
Peanut allergy, 125
Pediatricians, 9–10
Penis care, 145–46
Pets, 27–29
Phenylketonuria (PKU), 19
Phthalates, 176
Pigs (as surrogate mothers), 122
Plantain leaves, 106
Plants, toxic, 240
Play, 171–85. *See also* Games; Toys

benefits of, 172
   emotional milestones, 181–85
   social milestones, 179–81
Playdates, 179–80
Playgroups, 180–81
Play stations, 178–79
Pool safety, 241
Porcupines, 223
Private parts (hygiene), 144–46
Prolactin, 60
Pulling up, 245–46

Rabbits, 215
Rashes, 164, 167–69
Reading aloud, 233–34
Reproductive ectogenesis, 122
Restaurants, 197–99
Reye's syndrome, 165
Rice cereal, 112–13
Rocking, 36, 46–47
Rolling over, 30, 31, 243–44
Room, infant's, 7–8
Roseola, 167, 168

Safety. *See also* Babyproofing;
   Childproofing; Choking hazards
   bottle-feeding, 78
   feeding, 120–21
   at home, 29–32
   top ten household dangers, 14
   toy, 175–76
Savannah, Jaya, 133
Scheduled awakenings, 42
Seahorses, 241
Sears, Dr., 40
Separation anxiety, 184–85
Shakes, 162
Shoulder/upright hold, 20–21
Sign language, 228–33
Simethicone (Mylanta, Mylicon),
   51–52
Sitting up, 244
Skin-to-skin contact, 47, 58
Sleep, 33–42
   co-, 40
   parental, 26–27, 37–38
   patterns, establishing, 34–35
   patterns, explained, 33
   techniques for inducing, 35–37
   training methods, 39–42
Sleepiness, excessive, 163
Sling, constructing, 190–93
Smiles, 182
Smoke, secondhand, 11–12, 32

Smoke detectors, 12
Social milestones, 179–81
Solid foods, 109–27
    the body's preparation for, 110
    determining readiness for, 111
    first, 112–13
    gear for, 113–14
    instructions for feeding/serving,
        114–16
    second, 116–18
Soy-based formula, 52, 82–83
Squirrels, 99
Stiff neck, 163
Storks, 201
Stranger anxiety, 183–84
Sudden Infant Death Syndrome
    (SIDS), 12, 31–32
Sunglasses, 215–16
Sunscreen, 214
Suppositories, 167
Swaddling, 48–50
Swipe & grab, 243

Tasmanian devils, 65
Teething, 153–54
Teething biscuits, 131
Temperature, taking, 158–59
Tests (for newborns), 18–19
Thrush, 70–71
Tongue extrusion reflex, 110
Tonic neck reflex, 243
Tooth care, 154–56
Toys, 136, 143, 172–76, 203, 211,
    216
Travel and excursions, 187–217. *See
    also* Airplane travel; Automobile
    travel
    international, 213
    places to go, 195–202
    supplies for, 188–90, 204–5
    vacation choices, 204–5

Umbilical cord stump, 100, 146–47
Urinary tract infections, 92, 144, 146
Urination, 91–93

Vaccines, 19, 28
Vaginal discharge, bloody, 92–93
Vegetables, 132
Vegetarian/vegan diet, 82, 123–24
Vinegar, 106
Vitamin K, 19
Vomiting, 66, 160, 162, 163

Walkers, avoiding, 241
Walking, 246–47
Water
    hot water heater temperature, 11
    lead in, 13–14
Weissbluth, Marc, 41
Wheat-based foods, 112
Window blind cords, 240
Work
    sources of lead in, 14
    taking time from, 25–26

Yale University, 63
Yeast infections, 104, 106